The Ultimate Halloween Trivia Book
2nd Edition

The Ultimate Halloween Trivia Book
2nd Edition

by

Scotty McCoy

with editing by

Dylan Patton

and

Marcus Moutra

and a foreword by

Jamie Lee Curtis

Published by Kindle Direct Publishing

ISBN: 9781728661049

Dedicated to my dad, Scott G. McCoy, who, on September 14, 2016, was diagnosed with a rare, aggressive form of brain cancer known as Glioblastoma. As of November 23, 2016, he was told that he has beaten cancer after brain surgery, radiation, and chemotherapy and I am glad to announce to the world that my dad is cancer free. I love you dad. I knew you could do it!

Foreword

I was new to filming. I hadn't filmed anything prior. I got the role because of my mom, Janet Leigh, who was in the 1960 slasher film *Psycho*, and I was nervous to film my first movie that was also a slasher. After the first day of filming, I got a call from John Carpenter. I was terrified he was going to fire me. After all, I was a new actress with no prior experience and I felt like my first day on set wasn't good. I met with John and he told me I did a terrific job on set for the first day of filming and the rest was history. We made history. *Halloween* made history. We have ten films in the *Halloween* franchise and it is all because of a genius film director, John Carpenter.

A group of young adults who weren't that experienced with acting as the main cast. There was myself, along with Nancy Kyes and P.J. Soles as the main stars. Then there was Donald Pleasence, God bless his soul. Unfortunately, Donald has passed away, however, he was a major reason for *Halloween*'s success. If it weren't for John Carpenter spending extra money on Donald, I don't know if *Halloween* would've been a huge success. Then there was Brian Andrews and Kyle Richards, who played the two kids being babysat. They were tremendous child actors and they brought in the element of spookiness of Michael Myers: no one is safe, not even children. Charles Cyphers was great as well. He was a great actor who brought the feeling that Donald's character was crazy, but he also might be right.

Michael Myers, as a character, is supposed to be this evil human being that doesn't care who or what he kills. John Carpenter, along with the signature theme song, made Michael into a historical figure every October and a legendary, iconic character that is everyone's dream to be for Halloween. Debra Hill, who dated John back during filming, who unfortunately passed away from cancer, was the first ever Michael Myers. Many people say Will Sandin is, which he was Michael as a boy, but Debra Hill played Michael's arm when grabbing for the kitchen knife. So I have to give her credit where credit is due.

The entire cast and crew is ultimately responsible for *Halloween*'s success, and without *Halloween*, my career would've never even begun. Filming the original in 1978 was a great experience that had me in three of the ten sequels, and then it branched my career into multiple films, including *The Fog*, *Prom Night*, and even Fox's *Scream Queens*.

I want to thank Scotty for reaching out to me to write the foreword to his book, *The Ultimate Halloween Trivia Book*, because this franchise is so successful that it deserves an ultimate book for the ultimate fans. Without the fans, my career never would've taken off to begin with. I could've been in a movie that was a bust, but the fans made the movie so successful that Halloween has never been the same again.

Much love,

Jamie Lee Curtis
Actress, Author, and Philanthropist

Table of Contents

Foreword iv

Halloween (1978) 1

Halloween 2 (1981) 11

Halloween 3: Season of the Witch 22

Halloween 4: The Return of Michael Myers 33

Halloween 5: The Revenge of Michael Myers 43

Halloween: The Curse of Michael Myers 54

Halloween H20: 20 Years Later 65

Halloween: Resurrection 76

Halloween (2007) 87

Halloween 2 (2009) 98

Halloween (2018) 110

Halloween Mashup 122

Answer Key 136

Halloween (1978)

1. Who was the killer of *Halloween*?
    a. Jason Voorhees
    b. Michael Myers
    c. Freddy Krueger
    d. Mrs. Voorhees

2. Who directed *Halloween*?
    a. Debra Hill
    b. Wes Craven
    c. Sean S. Cunningham
    d. John Carpenter

3. What year did Michael kill Judith?
    a. 1963
    b. 1964
    c. 1965
    d. 1962

4. Who played Michael Myers?
    a. Nick Castle
    b. Christopher Durand
    c. Dick Warlock
    d. George P. Wilbur

5. Who was the final girl of *Halloween*?
    a. Annie Brackett
    b. Lynda Van Der Klok
    c. Laurie Strode
    d. Jamie Lloyd

6. Who played Dr. Sam Loomis?
    a. Charles Cyphers
    b. John Saxon
    c. Donald Pleasence
    d. Peter Boyle

7. What was the budget of *Halloween*?
    a. $550,000
    b. $275,000
    c. $300,000
    d. $425,000

8. What did *Halloween* make at the box office?
    a. $75,000,000
    b. $70,000,000
    c. $50,000,000
    d. $25,000,000

9. How old was Michael when he killed Judith?
    a. Five
    b. Twelve
    c. Seven
    d. Six

10. When was *Halloween* released into theaters?
    a. October 31, 1978
    b. October 30, 1978
    c. October 25, 1978
    d. October 28, 1978

11. What was the body count in *Halloween*?
    a. Six
    b. Five
    c. Three
    d. Four

12. What is the address of the Myers house?
    a. 45 Lampkin Lane   c. 43 Lampkin Lane
    b. 50 Lampkin Lane   d. 47 Lampkin Lane

13. What was the tagline for *Halloween*?
    a. The Night HE Came Home   c. The Night When HE Came Home
    b. The Night HE Returned Home   d. The Night HE Came Home to Kill

14. What does Lynda say when she reveals her breasts to Michael Myers, thinking he was Bob?
    a. See anything you like   c. See anything you want
    b. See anything you would like to touch   d. See anything you need

15. What was the story of Michael Myers?
    a. Yeah, you know every town has something like this happen... I remember over in
    Russellville, old Charlie Bowles, about fifteen years ago... One night, he finished dinner, and
    he excused himself from the table. He went out to the garage, and got himself a hacksaw.
    Then he went back into the house, kissed his wife and his two children goodbye, and then he
    proceeded to...
    b. I- I- I watched him for fifteen years, sitting in a room, staring at a wall, not seeing the
    wall, looking past the wall - looking at this night, inhumanly patient, waiting for some secret,
    silent alarm to trigger him off. Death has come to your little town, Sheriff. Now you can
    either ignore it, or you can help me to stop it.
    c. I met him, fifteen years ago; I was told there was nothing left; no reason, no conscience, no
    understanding; and even the most rudimentary sense of life or death, of good or evil, right or
    wrong. I met this six-year-old child, with this blank, pale, emotionless face, and the blackest
    eyes... the devil's eyes. I spent eight years trying to reach him, and then another seven trying
    to keep him locked up because I realized that what was living behind that boy's eyes was
    purely and simply... evil.
    d. He was my patient for fifteen years. He became an obsession with me until I realized that
    there was nothing within him, neither conscious nor reason that was... even remotely human.
    An hour ago I stood up and fired six shots into him and then he just got up and walked away.
    I am talking about the real possibility that he is STILL OUT THERE!

16. Who was Annie babysitting?
    a. Tommy Doyle   c. Lindsay Wallace
    b. Jamie Lloyd   d. Lonnie Elam

17. Jamie Lee Curtis is the daughter of Janet Leigh. Janet is known for her role in what horror
film?
    a. Psycho   c. Rosemary's Baby
    b. The Birds   d. Night of the Living Dead

18. What does Lynda do as an extracurricular activity in school?
    a. Softball   c. Cheerleading
    b. Basketball   d. Volleyball

19. What is the name of the mental hospital where Michael Myers was locked up?
    a. Samson's Grove Sanitarium   c. Smith's Grove Sanitarium
    b. Scott's Grove Sanitarium   d. Simpson's Grove Sanitarium

20. What was the setting of *Halloween*?
    a. Chicago, Illinois   c. Springfield, Illinois
    b. Bloomington, Illinois   d. Haddonfield, Illinois

21. What Halloween costume did Michael Myers wear when he killed his sister?
    a. Vampire   c. Magician
    b. Clown   d. Police Officer

22. When Sheriff Brackett scared Laurie, what does he say?
    a. It's Halloween, everyone is entitled to one good jump
    b. It's Halloween, everyone is entitled to one good scare
    c. It's Halloween, everyone is entitled to one good scream
    d. It's Halloween, everyone is entitled to one good fright

23. Which book did Laurie forget at school?
    a. Math   c. Chemistry
    b. English   d. History

24. What was Annie and Laurie smoking in the car?
    a. Cigarette   c. Marijuana
    b. Pipe   d. Cigar

25. What character name is Michael Myers credited as?
    a. The Figure   c. The Shape
    b. The Illusion   d. The Evil

26. What is the name of the nurse who works with Dr. Loomis?
    a. Marion Kaufman   c. Marion Klingerman
    b. Marion Billings   d. Marion Chambers

27. How many times did Dr. Loomis shoot Michael?
    a. Six   c. Five
    b. Three   d. Four

28. What name was on the matchbox?
    a. Red Rooster Lounge   c. Red Robin Lounge
    b. Red Rabbit Lounge   d. Red Roadrunner Lounge

29. Who created the famous theme song of *Halloween*?
    a. Debra Hill   c. John Carpenter
    b. Harry Manfredini   d. Moustapha Akkad

30. Who played the arm of Michael Myers when he killed his sister?
    a. Ari Lehman   c. Will Sandin
    b. Debra Hill   d. Malek Akkad

31. Every time Tommy sees Michael Myers; what does he say he saw?
    a. Michael Myers   c. A Monster
    b. The Boogeyman   d. A Stalker

32. Who did Laurie say she'd rather go to the prom with?
    a. Ben Tramer   c. Ted Hollister
    b. Paul Freedman   d. Bob Simms

33. Who wrote the *Halloween* screenplay?
    a. John Carpenter and Moustapha Akkad
    b. John Carpenter and Donald Pleasence
    c. John Carpenter and Debra Hill
    d. John Carpenter and Nick Castle

34. Who did Annie say was staring at Laurie?
    a. Mr. Riddle   c. Michael Myers
    b. Ben Tramer   d. Mr. Strode

35. Who was the doctor that Dr. Loomis was speaking to about Michael's escape?
    a. Dr. Wynn   c. Dr. Mixter
    b. Dr. Hoffman   d. Dr. Whale

36. How many dogs did Michael Myers kill?
    a. Three   c. One
    b. Two   d. None

37. What four textbooks did Lynda say she always forgets?
    a. Chemistry, Math, English, and Spanish
    b. Chemistry, Math, English, and German
    c. Chemistry, Math, English, and French
    d. Chemistry, Math, English, and Latin

38. Who played the voice of Paul?
    a. John Carpenter   c. Tony Moran
    b. Nick Castle   d. David Kyle

39. Who was Laurie babysitting?
    a. Tommy Doyle   c. Lindsay Wallace
    b. Jamie Lloyd   d. Lonnie Elam

40. What does Laurie's father do for a living?
    a. Realtor   c. Banker
    b. Insurance Agent   d. Businessman

41. What three comic books did Tommy have that Laurie looked at?
    a. Laser Man, Neutron Man, and Arachnid Man
    b. Laser Man, Neutron Man, and Tarantula Man
    c. Laser Man, Neutron Man, and Anaconda Man
    d. Laser Man, Neutron Man, and Cobra Man

42. Who did Annie say Ben Tramer went out drinking with?
    a. Paul Freedman   c. Bob Simms
    b. Mike Godfrey   d. Bud Scarlotti

43. How old is Mr. Riddle?
    a. 88   c. 85
    b. 89   d. 87

44. Who did Lynda think was driving the car Michael Myers was driving?
    a. Ben Tramer   c. Devon Graham
    b. Paul Freedman   d. Mike Godfrey

45. What does Dr. Loomis always call Michael Myers?
    a. Satan   c. Evil
    b. Devil   d. Demon

46. What did Annie spill on her clothes?
    a. Wine   c. Beer
    b. Butter   d. Juice

47. What was the name of Lindsay's dog?
    a. Lester   c. Max
    b. Sundae   d. Muffin

48. What does Annie hate in a guy that drives?
    a. No Sense of Humor   c. No Personality
    b. No Style   d. No Intelligence

49. What horror film was Lindsay watching while Annie was babysitting her?
    a. Psycho   c. The Thing
    b. The Texas Chainsaw Massacre   d. Young Frankenstein

50. What did Annie say kills when she yelled at the car Michael Myers was driving?
    a. Acid   c. Speed
    b. Ecstasy   d. Crack

51. Who did Annie say Laurie should ask to the dance?
    a. Ben Tramer   c. Dick Baxter
    b. Devon Graham   d. Mike Godfrey

52. What two things did Annie say she plans on doing with Lindsay Wallace?
    a. Eating Popcorn and Watching The Thing
    b. Eating Popcorn and Watching Psycho
    c. Eating Popcorn and Watching Dracula
    d. Eating Popcorn and Watching Dr. Dementia

53. Annie said Laurie would always make a fabulous what?
    a. Babysitter   c. Cheerleader
    b. Girl Scout   d. Housewife

54. Who was Michael Myers' sister that he killed as a child?
    a. Judith Myers   c. Joan Myers
    b. Jenny Myers   d. Jillian Myers

55. What was taken from the cemetery by Michael Myers that showed he is back to finish what he started?
    a. Judith's Tombstone   c. Judith's Flowers
    b. Judith's Corpse   d. Judith's Casket

56. What did Lynda tell Bob to get her after they finished making love?
    a. Beer   c. Soda
    b. Juice   d. Water

57. What was stolen from the store?
    a. Halloween Masks, Knives, and Guns
    b. Halloween Masks, Knives, and Rope
    c. Halloween Masks, Knives, and Newspapers
    d. Halloween Masks, Knives, and Candy

58. What was the name of Judith's boyfriend that was seen in the beginning of *Halloween*?
    a. Donald Hodges   c. Daniel Hodges
    b. Derek Hodges   d. Dillon Hodges

59. What were the names of Michael's parents?
    a. Derrick and Ellen Myers   c. Donald and Edith Myers
    b. Darren and Edna Myers   d. Dennis and Eleanor Myers

60. Who did Michael kill on his way to Haddonfield?
    a. Train Conductor   c. Truck Driver
    b. Mechanic   d. Hitchhiker

61. What was Tommy holding in his arms when he was being bullied at school?
    a. Textbooks
    b. Halloween Mask
    c. Candy
    d. Pumpkin

62. What was the name of the store that was robbed?
    a. Noonan's Hardware Store
    b. Nightingale's Hardware Store
    c. Nicholson's Hardware Store
    d. Nichol's Hardware Store

63. How does Michael kill Lester?
    a. Kicks Him
    b. Breaks His Neck
    c. Stabs Him
    d. Strangles Him

64. What was the first name of the kid that Dr. Loomis whispered to get away from the Myers house?
    a. Lance
    b. Larry
    c. Lenny
    d. Lonnie

65. When Lynda calls Laurie and Michael begins choking her, Laurie thinks it is Annie calling her. Laurie said to her alright Annie, first I get your famous chewing now I get your famous what?
    a. Screeching
    b. Screaming
    c. Squealing
    d. Squeaking

66. Who did Sheriff Brackett blame on robbing the store?
    a. Michael Myers
    b. Thieves
    c. Kids
    d. Lynda and Bob

67. *Halloween* is classified as what kind of horror film?
    a. Psychological Thriller
    b. Mentally Emotional Mystery
    c. Sociological Suspense
    d. Sophisticated Slasher

68. What state has a Haddonfield in it that is inspiration for the naming of the fictitious town?
    a. Pennsylvania
    b. California
    c. New Jersey
    d. New York

69. Who played the role of Lynda Van Der Klok?
    a. Nancy Loomis
    b. P.J. Soles
    c. Jamie Lee Curtis
    d. Kyle Richards

70. After Michael Myers was shot by Dr. Loomis, what happened to him to end the film?
    a. He was gone
    b. He died
    c. He sat up
    d. He walked away

71. Whose corpse did Michael have on the bed with his sister's tombstone above the corpse?
    a. Lynda Van Der Klok
    b. Bob Simms
    c. Annie Brackett
    d. Judith's Corpse

72. Whose house did Laurie tell Tommy and Lindsay to go to and call for help?
    a. McKenzie's   c. McCoy's
    b. McCormick's   d. McDonald's

73. Who played the role of Sheriff Brackett?
    a. Donald Pleasence   c. Charles Cyphers
    b. Brian Andrews   d. John Michael Graham

74. What did Laurie say she was going to do with Tommy?
    a. Watch Horror Movies   c. Go Trick-or-Treating
    b. Play Pranks   d. Carve Jack-o'-Lanterns

75. What did Laurie say to herself when she saw Tommy trick-or-treating?
    a. I thought you outgrew Halloween
    b. I thought you outgrew superstition
    c. I thought you outgrew tradition
    d. I thought you outgrew trick-or-treating

76. What were the names of the actor and actress to play the roles of Tommy Doyle and Lindsay
Wallace?
    a. Brian Andrews and Kyle Richards
    b. John Michael Graham and P.J. Soles
    c. Donald Pleasence and Jamie Lee Curtis
    d. Charles Cyphers and Nancy Loomis

77. Who played the role of Annie Brackett?
    a. Sandy Johnson   c. P.J. Soles
    b. Nancy Kyes   d. Jamie Lee Curtis

78. What word did Lynda always say?
    a. Radical   c. Dude
    b. Totally   d. Definitely

79. Why did Lynda tell Bob to not rip her blouse?
    a. It was a rare piece of clothing   c. It was expensive
    b. It was her grandmother's   d. It was her favorite blouse

80. What time did Lynda say to Laurie that the dance started?
    a. 9:00 PM   c. 8:00 PM
    b. 7:00 PM   d. 10:00 PM

81. Where did Paul drag Annie into to tell her he has been grounded?
    a. Janitor's Closet   c. Locker Room
    b. His Van   d. Boy's Bathroom

82. Where did Annie get stuck when she was washing her clothes?
    a. In the laundry room's window   c. In between the washer and dryer
    b. Underneath the door when it fell on her   d. She didn't get stuck

83. What did Annie say Lester found when he stopped barking?
    a. Someone else to hate   c. A dog bone
    b. A way into the house   d. A hot date

84. Who played the role of Bob Simms?
    a. John Michael Graham   c. Brian Andrews
    b. Nick Castle   d. Donald Pleasence

85. What did Michael kill Judith with?
    a. A pair of scissors   c. A fork
    b. A glass shard   d. A kitchen knife

86. What did Sheriff Brackett say could've eaten the dog in the Myers house?
    a. Skunk   c. Rat
    b. Opossum   d. Birds

87. What did Laurie stab Michael in the neck with in the living room?
    a. Knife   c. Clothes Hanger
    b. Knitting Needle   d. Fork

88. What did Laurie call Annie and Lynda in the following sentence: Alright __________ joke's over?
    a. Pranksters   c. Morons
    b. Meatheads   d. Idiots

89. What was the song lyric that Laurie sang when she dropped the key off at the Myers house?
    a. We all live in the yellow submarine
    b. Hello, is it me you're looking for
    c. I wish I had you all alone, just the two of us
    d. Who you gonna call, ghostbusters

90. How many miles away did Dr. Wynn tell Dr. Loomis Haddonfield was from Smith's Grove?
    a. 100 Miles   c. 150 Miles
    b. 200 Miles   d. 250 Miles

91. What grade did Laurie tell Tommy that Lonnie Elam probably won't get out of?
    a. 4th Grade   c. 5th Grade
    b. 6th Grade   d. 7th Grade

92. What did Laurie tell the teacher that Samuels thought fate was like?
    a. Religion   c. Politics
    b. Historical   d. Natural Element

93. Who played Michael Myers as a child in the beginning of the film?
    a. Erik Preston   c. Billy Warlock
    b. Adam Gunn   d. Will Sandin

94. What is Michael Myers' birthday?
    a. October 31, 1957   c. October 30, 1957
    b. October 19, 1957   d. October 2, 1957

95. After Dr. Loomis shot Michael, Michael fell off of what?
    a. Porch   c. Balcony
    b. Steps   d. Roof

96. As the movie ended, what could be heard of Michael's that signified that he was still alive?
    a. Michael's deep breathing   c. Michael laughing
    b. Michael humming the Halloween theme song   d. Michael groaning and moaning

97. How did Laurie free herself from being strangled by Michael?
    a. Stabbing him in the neck with his knife   c. Unmasking him
    b. Dr. Loomis showed up and distracted him   d. Stabbed him in the eye

98. Who played Michael Myers during the closet scene?
    a. Nick Castle   c. John Carpenter
    b. Tony Moran   d. Tommy Lee Wallace

99. What is Michael's middle name?
    a. Audrey   c. Allan
    b. Andrew   d. Albert

100. Who played the role of Laurie Strode?
    a. P.J. Soles   c. Jamie Lee Curtis
    b. Sandy Johnson   d. Nancy Loomis

Halloween 2 (1981)

1. What is the story of Samhain as told by Dr. Loomis?
   a. He was my patient for fifteen years. He became an obsession with me until I realized that there was nothing within him, neither conscious nor reason that was... even remotely human. An hour ago I stood up and fired six shots into him and then he just got up and walked away. I am talking about the real possibility that he is STILL OUT THERE!
   b. I- I- I watched him for fifteen years, sitting in a room, staring at a wall, not seeing the wall, looking past the wall - looking at this night, inhumanly patient, waiting for some secret, silent alarm to trigger him off. Death has come to your little town, Sheriff. Now you can either ignore it, or you can help me to stop it.
   c. In order to appease the gods, the Druid priests held fire rituals. Prisoners of war, criminals, the insane, animals... were... burned alive in baskets. By observing the way they died, the Druids believed they could see omens of the future. Two thousand years later, we've come no further. Samhain isn't evil spirits. It isn't goblins, ghosts or witches. It's the unconscious mind. We're all afraid of the dark inside ourselves.
   d. I met him, fifteen years ago; I was told there was nothing left; no reason, no conscience, no understanding; and even the most rudimentary sense of life or death, of good or evil, right or wrong. I met this six-year-old child, with this blank, pale, emotionless face, and the blackest eyes... the devil's eyes. I spent eight years trying to reach him, and then another seven trying to keep him locked up because I realized that what was living behind that boy's eyes was purely and simply... evil.

2. Who was the final girl of *Halloween 2*?
   a. Jill Franco
   b. Janet Marshall
   c. Laurie Strode
   d. Karen Bailey

3. What was the name of the hospital?
   a. Haddonfield General
   b. Haddonfield Clinic
   c. Haddonfield Memorial Hospital
   d. Haddonfield University Hospital

4. What was the budget of *Halloween 2*?
   a. $2.3 million
   b. $2.7 million
   c. $2.5 million
   d. $2.9 million

5. Who directed *Halloween 2*?
   a. Debra Hill
   b. John Carpenter
   c. Rick Rosenthal
   d. Tommy Lee Wallace

6. When was *Halloween 2* released into theaters?
   a. October 30, 1981
   b. October 29, 1981
   c. October 31, 1981
   d. October 25, 1981

7. What was the name of Laurie's father?
   a. Michael Strode
   b. Morgan Strode
   c. Matthew Strode
   d. Mason Strode

8. Which of the following actresses portrayed Nurse Jill Franco?
    a. Pamela Susan Shoop   c. Ana Alicia
    b. Gloria Gifford   d. Tawny Moyer

9. What are the names of the two EMTs that took Laurie to the hospital?
    a. Gary Hunt and Leigh Brackett
    b. Jimmy Lloyd and Budd Scarlotti
    c. Frederick Mixter and Ben Tramer
    d. Sam Loomis and Mr. Garrett

10. Which character on *Days of our Lives* did the young boy that was holding the boom box portray years after the release of *Halloween 2*?
    a. Max Brady   c. Frankie Brady
    b. Shawn Douglas Brady   d. Rex Brady

11. How old is Michael Myers?
    a. Twenty   c. Twenty-Two
    b. Twenty-One   d. Twenty-Three

12. Who was the dentist that was checking the teeth and gums of the charred corpse?
    a. Gabriel   c. Gerry
    b. Graham   d. Garrison

13. In the beginning of the film, which character from the first film's neighbor went to check what the commotion was after Dr. Loomis shot Michael Myers?
    a. Lindsay Wallace   c. Annie Brackett
    b. Laurie Strode   d. Tommy Doyle

14. When Jimmy brought Laurie to the hospital, where did Nurse Jill say Dr. Mixter was at?
    a. Country Club   c. His Office
    b. Halloween Party   d. Staff Meeting

15. In the television version of the film, the Marshall wasn't killed with his throat slit like in the theater version of the film, but was killed how?
    a. Stabbed in the back   c. Stabbed in the stomach
    b. Stabbed in the eye   d. Stabbed in the chest

16. What did Jimmy slip on when he was looking for help in finding Laurie?
    a. Water   c. Blood
    b. Juice   d. Floor Wax

17. Who does Karen give a ride home to before she goes to work at the hospital?
    a. Debra   c. Dina
    b. Dora   d. Darcy

18. According to Karen, where is Eddie Lee at?
    a. Chicago   c. Russellville
    b. Springfield   d. Smith's Grove

19. Who did the governor send with the Marshall to find Dr. Loomis just in case he found
Michael Myers?
    a. Dr. Wynn   c. Dr. Mixter
    b. Dr. Hoffman   d. Marion Chambers

20. Which doctor from Smith's Grove Sanitarium is afraid the melee caused by Michael Myers
will jeopardize the whole rehabilitation program?
    a. Dr. Mixter   c. Dr. Wynn
    b. Dr. Rogers   d. Dr. Hoffman

21. Of the characters killed in the first film, which character's corpse is shown in *Halloween 2*?
    a. Lynda Van Der Klok   c. Annie Brackett
    b. Judith Myers   d. Bob Simms

22. Nurse Janet said who saw Michael Myers when coming to work?
    a. Jenna   c. Julie
    b. Joanie   d. Jessica

23. Which of the following actresses portrayed Nurse Karen Bailey?
    a. Gloria Gifford   c. Tawny Moyer
    b. Pamela Susan Shoop   d. Ana Alicia

24. Who was mistaken for Michael Myers, got killed, and was later revealed to not have been
Michael?
    a. Eddie Lee   c. Ben Tramer
    b. Mike Godfrey   d. Paul Freedman

25. What did Bud tell Jimmy the first rule about being a paramedic is?
    a. Never get involved with nurses
    b. Never get involved with killers
    c. Never get involved with coworkers
    d. Never get involved with patients

26. What did *Halloween 2* make at the box office?
    a. $25.5 million   c. $25.1 million
    b. $25.2 million   d. $25.8 million

27. Whose body did Jimmy find when he slipped?
    a. Mrs. Alves   c. Mr. Garrett
    b. Nurse Jill Franco   d. Dr. Mixter

28. Where did Nurse Janet say Julie saw Michael Myers at?
    a. Behind the Haddonfield Drive In
    b. Behind the Lost River Drive In
    c. Behind the Halloween Memorial Drive In
    d. Behind the Haddonfield Outskirts Drive In

29. Which of the following actresses portrayed the head nurse of the hospital, Mrs. Alves?
    a. Tawny Moyer   c. Gloria Gifford
    b. Ana Alicia   d. Pamela Susan Shoop

30. In this television version of the film, who is revealed to be alive and okay in the hospital with Laurie Strode?
    a. Sam Loomis   c. Jimmy Lloyd
    b. Mrs. Alves   d. Dr. Mixter

31. What was the last name of the elderly couple in the beginning of the film?
    a. Englewood   c. Emery
    b. Everett   d. Elrod

32. What did Dr. Loomis say Samhain translated to?
    a. Lord of the Sacrifices   c. Lord of the Rituals
    b. Lord of the Dead   d. Lord of the Night

33. What is the name of Jimmy's brother?
    a. Zachary   c. Ziggy
    b. Zeke   d. Zorro

34. What two substances does Dr. Loomis fill the room with as a distraction to allow Laurie to escape right before he blew the room up?
    a. Ether and Oxygen Gas
    b. Ether and Carbon Monoxide
    c. Ether and Helium
    d. Ether and Carbon Dioxide

35. Who did Michael first kill in *Halloween 2*?
    a. Alice Martin   c. Mr. Garrett
    b. Nurse Karen Bailey   d. Nurse Janet Marshall

36. What major twist was introduced in this film?
    a. Michael Myers is controlled by the curse of the thorn
    b. Michael Myers can only be stopped, but never killed
    c. Michael Myers is the brother of Laurie Strode
    d. Michael Myers is only able to kill on Halloween night

37. Which of the following actors portrayed Michael Myers?
    a. Nick Castle   c. Tom Morga
    b. Dick Warlock   d. Christopher Durand

38. Which television sitcom was the actor who played Dr. Mixter a recurring character on years after the release of *Halloween 2*?
    a. Seinfeld   c. Everybody Loves Raymond
    b. The King of Queens   d. Friends

39. What is the date that the film is set in?
    a. October 31, 1981   c. October 31, 1978
    b. October 31, 1980   d. October 31, 1979

40. What did Dr. Mixter have in his eye that described the way Michael killed him?
    a. Scalpel   c. Syringe
    b. Pen   d. Nail

41. Which of the following actresses portrayed Nurse Janet Marshall?
    a. Ana Alicia   c. Pamela Susan Shoop
    b. Tawny Moyer   d. Gloria Gifford

42. After Sheriff Brackett is given time to grieve after the death of his daughter, who is put in charge of finding Michael Myers?
    a. Gary Hunt   c. Dr. Loomis
    b. The Governor   d. The Marshall

43. When Sheriff Brackett said to Dr. Loomis that he let Michael Myers out, Dr. Loomis responded by saying he didn't let him out but gave orders for him to be what?
    a. Committed   c. Evaluated
    b. Confined   d. Restrained

44. The first patrolman told Gary Hunt that the Myers House is empty and he also covered all of what part of town?
    a. North   c. South
    b. East   d. West

45. Upon seeing Karen, Budd sang his version of what song?
    a. Amazing Grace   c. Purple Rain
    b. Call Me Maybe   d. Jailhouse Rock

46. Dr. Mixter asks Nurse Janet Marshall to get him some more what?
    a. Bandages   c. Donuts
    b. Coffee   d. Syringes

47. Karen told Darcy to go ask who for a ride?
    a. Ben Tramer   c. Alice Martin
    b. Eddie Lee   d. Janet Marshall

48. When Michael Myers killed Nurse Janet Marshall, what did it cause in her brain by injecting her with a syringe of air?
    a. Aneurysm   c. Embolism
    b. Catheter   d. Immobilization

49. What did Michael Myers burn and eventually drown Karen in?
    a. Swimming Pool   c. Shower
    b. Therapy Tub   d. Jacuzzi

50. How did Michael Myers kill Mrs. Alves?
    a. He slit her throat with a scalpel
    b. He strapped her to a surgical table and drained her blood with a catheter
    c. He filled her head with air from a syringe
    d. He hit her in the head with the claw of a hammer

51. Whose corpse did Laurie Strode find?
    a. Dr. Mixter   c. Mrs. Alves
    b. Mr. Garrett   d. Nurse Karen Bailey

52. What jumped out of the dumpster when Mr. Garrett was looking for a trespasser?
    a. Rabbit   c. Cat
    b. Dog   d. Rat

53. Who had the records of Laurie Strode sealed?
    a. Her parents   c. The court
    b. The Governor   d. The state

54. Nurse Jill Franco went to go get help but couldn't leave the hospital because why?
    a. The cars' tires were slashed and wouldn't start up
    b. The cars in the parking lot were damaged upon repair
    c. The cars' gas was completely drained
    d. The cars in the parking lot were vandalized and thus scared her back into the hospital

55. What did the dentist say the charred corpse had nothing of?
    a. Gum Disease   c. Cavities
    b. Damaged Nerves   d. Fillings

56. Laurie was going into a what that alerted Nurse Janet to go and find Dr. Mixter?
    a. Seizure   c. Coma
    b. Shock   d. Hypertension

57. What did Michael steal from the elderly couple?
    a. Sandwich   c. Radio
    b. Kitchen Knife   d. Halloween Mask

58. The actor who played Michael Myers in *Halloween 2* also played what other minor role in the film?
    a. Medic   c. Patrolman #3
    b. Announcer   d. Producer

59. What was the name of the kid with the boom box?
    a. Randy   c. Tommy
    b. Craig   d. Billy

60. What was the tagline for *Halloween 2*?
    a. The Continuation of the Night HE Came Home
    b. The Second Part of the Night HE Came Home
    c. More of the Night HE Came Home
    d. The Aftermath of the Night HE Came Home

61. Who were the two producers of *Halloween 2*?
    a. John Carpenter and Debra Hill
    b. Moustapha and Malek Akkad
    c. Rick Rosenthal and Tommy Lee Wallace
    d. Dean Cundey and Mark Goldblatt

62. What time did Ben Tramer leave the Halloween party when his friends came to Gary Hunt with concern of his whereabouts?
    a. 11:00 PM   c. 10:00 PM
    b. 9:00 PM   d. 12:00 AM

63. How many years has it been since the anniversary of Michael Myers killing his sister?
    a. Thirteen Years   c. Fifteen Years
    b. Ten Years   d. Sixteen Years

64. How old did Gary Hunt say he was the night Michael Myers killed his sister?
    a. Fifteen   c. Thirteen
    b. Fourteen   d. Sixteen

65. As Laurie is in the ambulance and being taken away, what was she having flashbacks of?
    a. Michael Myers attacking her   c. The bodies of her friends
    b. Michael Myers' burning body   d. Dr. Loomis shooting Michael

66. When Gary Hunt asks the patrolman what the count is so far, what number does he respond with?
    a. Eleven   c. Nine
    b. Ten   d. Thirteen

67. Which child actor played Michael Myers as a young boy in *Halloween 2*?
    a. Brian Andrews   c. Will Sandin
    b. Adam Gunn   d. Billy Warlock

68. Where does the film start off?
    a. Laurie Strode being rushed to the hospital
    b. Michael Myers escaping into a dark alley
    c. Directly after the end of the first film
    d. Dr. Loomis calling the police

69. What is similar about the death of Mr. Garrett in *Halloween 2* compared to the death of Deputy Winslow in *Friday the 13th Part 2*?
    a. Both are officers of the law that were killed with a hammer claw to the head
    b. Both are officers of the law that were driving cop cars before their death
    c. Both are officers of the law that found their killers' homes before they died
    d. Both are officers of the law that were killed and had their bodies part of the memorial for deceased family members

70. How late was Nurse Karen Bailey to work at the hospital?
    a. Ten Minutes   c. One Hour
    b. Fifteen Minutes   d. Thirty Minutes

71. Why did Mrs. Elrod scream?
    a. From the horror movie her husband was watching
    b. She saw blood on her cutting board
    c. Her husband was found dead
    d. There was a dead dog on her porch

72. What part of the hospital does Nurse Karen work in?
    a. Intensive Care Unit   c. Burn Center
    b. Coronary Care Unit   d. Maternity Ward

73. Where did Michael Myers leave clues at that Dr. Loomis ended up finding?
    a. Myers House   c. Elementary School
    b. Haddonfield Memorial Hospital   d. Police Station

74. How many times did Dr. Loomis shoot Michael in the hospital?
    a. Six   c. Five
    b. Four   d. Three

75. Where did Laurie shoot Michael when he wounded Dr. Loomis?
    a. In the head   c. In his eyes
    b. In the stomach   d. In the groin

76. What room in the hospital did Dr. Loomis and Laurie Strode lure Michael into for the official "kill"?
    a. Operating Room   c. Waiting Room
    b. Basement   d. Physical Therapy Room

77. Where did Laurie Strode run from Michael to narrowly escape him before heading to the parking lot?
    a. Boiler Room   c. Break Room
    b. Recovery Room   d. Cardiology Room

78. Who was wheeling Laurie Strode in the wheelchair towards the ambulance at the end of the film?
    a. Dr. Loomis   c. Gary Hunt
    b. Jimmy Lloyd   d. Marion Chambers

79. What did Michael Myers stab Nurse Jill Franco in the back with to kill her?
    a. Syringe   c. Scalpel
    b. Knife   d. Spear

80. What type of officer was Mr. Garrett?
    a. Police Officer   c. Security Guard
    b. Sheriff   d. Deputy

81. What made Dr. Loomis think that Ben Tramer was Michael Myers?
    a. He was walking like he was injured   c. He was wearing Michael's mask
    b. He had blood on his clothes   d. He was holding a knife

82. When Michael first arrives at the hospital, what does he do?
    a. Kill Mr. Garrett   c. Shut off the lights
    b. Cut the phone lines   d. Attack Laurie Strode

83. This film was supposed to be the last film to be about what?
    a. The last film of the Halloween franchise
    b. The last film based on Michael Myers and the town of Haddonfield
    c. The last film to feature Dr. Loomis
    d. The last film in the franchise to feature John Carpenter behind the scenes

84. Who ordered Dr. Loomis to be sent back to Smith's Grove?
    a. Marion Chambers   c. The Marshall
    b. The Governor   d. Dr. Wynn

85. What did Marion Chambers use to call for help to the hospital?
    a. The Marshall's Walkie Talkie   c. The Marshall's Two-Way Radio
    b. The Marshall's Phone   d. The Marshall's PDA

86. How does Dr. Loomis get The Marshall to turn around and drive to the hospital?
    a. Threatens to kill him   c. Fires a warning shot
    b. Blackmails him   d. Pleads him to help save Laurie

87. What are the last words that Dr. Loomis says to Michael before blowing them both up?
    a. Time to burn, Michael   c. It's time, Michael
    b. Go to Hell, Michael   d. Hell awaits, Michael

88. What type of gun does Dr. Loomis have on him during his hunt for Michael?
    a. Pistol   c. Revolver
    b. Rifle   d. Shotgun

89. What three curse words does Nurse Janet Marshall say Bud always says?
    a. Hell, shit, and damn   c. Ass, bitch, and bastard
    b. Fuck, Christ, and cunt   d. Slut, whore, and ho

90. What store by the mall did Janet say Julie saw Michael when she stopped by the light?
    a. Shop and Bag   c. Shop and Leave
    b. Shop and Pay   d. Shop and Stop

91. What does Dr. Loomis say to Gary Hunt about Michael being like some kind of animal?
    a. In order to appease the gods, the Druid priests held fire rituals. Prisoners of war, criminals,
    the insane, animals... were... burned alive in baskets. By observing the way they died, the
    Druids believed they could see omens of the future. Two thousand years later, we've come no
    further. Samhain isn't evil spirits. It isn't goblins, ghosts or witches. It's the unconscious
    mind. We're all afraid of the dark inside ourselves.
    b. He was my patient for fifteen years. He became an obsession with me until I realized that
    there was nothing within him, neither conscious nor reason that was... even remotely human.
    An hour ago I stood up and fired six shots into him and then he just got up and walked away.
    I am talking about the real possibility that he is STILL OUT THERE!
    c. I ought to handcuff you to the wheel, but I have a feeling I'm gonna need you in there. Can
    I trust you?
    d. I shot him 6 times! I shot him in the heart-but... HE'S NOT HUMAN!

92. What were the lyrics of Amazing Grace that Budd sang about Nurse Karen Bailey?
    a. Amazing Grace, give me no space / Don't make me cry / I tell no lie…
    b. Amazing Grace, wear leather and lace / Don't make me cry / I would die…
    c. Amazing Grace, I sense your trace / Don't make me cry / I'm a typical guy…
    d. Amazing Grace, come sit on my face / Don't make me cry / I need your pie...

93. What is Gary Hunt's rank with the Haddonfield Police Department?
    a. Sheriff   c. Officer
    b. Homicide Detective   d. Deputy

94. Why does Sheriff Brackett go off duty and put Gary Hunt in charge of finding Michael Myers with Dr. Loomis?
    a. To grieve the loss of his daughter, Annie
    b. To tell his wife of Annie's death
    c. To plan for Annie's funeral
    d. To find out why Michael killed Annie

95. What does Dr. Loomis tell Gary Hunt the gun does for him?
    a. It raises his guard
    b. It better prepares him
    c. It heightens his security
    d. It increased his protection

96. When Dr. Loomis asks if he can trust the Marshal, the Marshal responds by saying "What have I got to lose, except my ____________". What does he say is the only thing he can lose?
    a. Life
    b. License
    c. Job
    d. Dignity

97. How long does Karen tell Darcy it takes to get to her house and then back to the hospital?
    a. Five minutes
    b. Fifteen Minutes
    c. Ten Minutes
    d. Thirty Minutes

98. How long does Mrs. Alves give Jimmy to visit Laurie?
    a. Three Minutes
    b. Two Minutes
    c. Five Minutes
    d. Four Minutes

99. Where does Mr. Garrett think someone broke into?
    a. The Hospital
    b. The Ambulance
    c. The Storage Room
    d. The Myers House

100. Dr. Rogers doesn't want anyone from which department anywhere near Haddonfield?
    a. Psychiatric Department
    b. Therapeutic Department
    c. Health Department
    d. Rehabilitation Department

Halloween 3: Season of the Witch

1. Who directed *Halloween 3: Season of the Witch*?
    a. John Carpenter
    b. Dwight H. Little
    c. Debra Hill
    d. Tommy Lee Wallace

2. What was the name of the company that made the Halloween masks?
    a. Silver Shamrock Novelties
    b. Clever n' Evil Novelties
    c. Spooky Halloween Novelties
    d. All Hallows' Eve Novelties

3. What were the businessmen that were created by Conal Cochran?
    a. Cyborgs
    b. Androids
    c. Robots
    d. Zombies

4. What was the budget of *Halloween 3: Season of the Witch*?
    a. $2.2 million
    b. $2.7 million
    c. $2.5 million
    d. $2.9 million

5. What children's song does the commercial play its version of?
    a. Ring Around the Rosie
    b. Patty Cake
    c. London Bridges
    d. Mary Had a Little Lamb

6. When was *Halloween 3: Season of the Witch* released into theaters?
    a. October 30, 1982
    b. October 31, 1982
    c. October 22, 1982
    d. October 31, 1983

7. Who were the two producers of *Halloween 3: Season of the Witch*?
    a. John Carpenter and Debra Hill
    b. Debra Hill and Tommy Lee Wallace
    c. John Carpenter and Tommy Lee Wallace
    d. Moustapha and Malek Akkad

8. What do each of the masks have on it that will activate when a child wears the mask and watches the commercial?
    a. Microchip
    b. Antenna
    c. Battery
    d. Radio

9. What is the date in the beginning of the film?
    a. Friday, October 31, 1982
    b. Sunday, October 30, 1982
    c. Thursday, October 29, 1982
    d. Saturday, October 23, 1982

10. Harry Grimbridge is holding which of the Silver Shamrock masks in his hands?
    a. Witch
    b. Ghost
    c. Jack-o'-Lantern
    d. Skeleton

11. What is the city and state that is home to the Silver Shamrock Novelties?
    a. San Diego, California   c. Haddonfield, Illinois
    b. Santa Mira, California   d. Los Angeles, California

12. What does Marge Guttman recklessly poke the microchip with?
    a. Pen   c. Safety Pin
    b. Paperclip   d. Bobby Pin

13. Where does Harry Grimbridge collapse before being taken to the hospital?
    a. Gas Station   c. Highway
    b. Car Garage   d. Convenience Store

14. What is the first name of Harry's daughter?
    a. Ellen   c. Emily
    b. Ellie   d. Ella

15. What is the name of Dr. Daniel Challis' friend that does a lot of research for him?
    a. Teddy   c. Terri
    b. Tanya   d. Trish

16. What did Conal Cochran reveal about the way the children die when watching the
commercial wearing the Halloween masks?
    a. The children will die as sacrifices to the Old Gods, bringing about a ritual to appease them.
    b. The children will die as sacrifices to the Old Gods, bringing about a return of ancient
    Celtic rituals in celebration of Samhain.
    c. The children will die as sacrifices to the Old Gods, bringing about a resurrection of the
    ancient age of witchcraft.
    d. The children will die as sacrifices to the Old Gods, bringing about a rapture of all lost
    souls and spirits during the ancient times of Samhain custom practices.

17. Who from the original *Halloween* returned in this film as the ex-wife of Dr. Daniel Challis?
    a. Laurie Strode   c. Annie Brackett
    b. Lynda Van Der Klok   d. Marion Chambers

18. When Dr. Daniel Challis found the kidnapped Ellie Grimbridge, she turned out to be what?
    a. A Brainwashed Killer   c. A Hypnotized Zombie
    b. A Cloned Human   d. A Duplicated Android

19. What were the first names of Dr. Daniel Challis' children?
    a. Wally and Brenda   c. Wilbur and Billie
    b. Willie and Bella   d. Wallace and Betsy

20. Which behind the scene crew member played the role of the Silver Shamrock announcer on
the commercials?
    a. John Carpenter   c. Debra Hill
    b. Tommy Lee Wallace   d. Dean Cundey

21. What did *Halloween 3: Season of the Witch* make at the box office?
    a. $14.4 million
    b. $14.6 million
    c. $14 million
    d. $14.8 million

22. What were the three types of masks sold by Silver Shamrock Novelties?
    a. Vampire, Mummy, and Zombie
    b. Clown, Frankenstein, and Ghost
    c. Jack-o'-Lantern, Witch, and Skeleton
    d. Michael Myers, Wolf, and Devil

23. What does the microchips contain that causes the signal in the commercial to activate the microchip?
    a. Subliminal Messages
    b. Radio Waves
    c. Glass Fragments
    d. Stonehenge

24. What is the name of the gas station attendant that drove Harry Grimbridge to the hospital?
    a. William James
    b. Walter Jones
    c. Warner Jonas
    d. Wayne Johnson

25. What are the first names of the Kupfer family?
    a. Buddy, Betty, and Little Buddy
    b. Bernie, Beatrice, and Little Bernie
    c. Barry, Blanche, and Little Barry
    d. Barney, Bertha, and Little Barney

26. What is the name of Dr. Dan Challis' ex-wife?
    a. Lori
    b. Lorraine
    c. Lisa
    d. Linda

27. Who from the original *Halloween* film played an uncredited double role as both the curfew announcer and the telephone operator?
    a. Marion Chambers
    b. Laurie Strode
    c. Lynda Van Der Klok
    d. Annie Brackett

28. Which character from *Halloween 2* did the actor who played the Android Assassin in *Halloween 3: Season of the Witch* play?
    a. Gary Hunt
    b. Jimmy Lloyd
    c. Michael Myers
    d. Ben Tramer

29. What room number did Dr. Daniel Challis put Harry Grimbridge in?
    a. Thirty-One
    b. Eighteen
    c. Thirteen
    d. Twenty-One

30. What time does the "big giveaway" take place according to the commercial?
    a. 9:00 PM
    b. 10:00 PM
    c. 11:00 PM
    d. 12:00 AM

31. Where was Harry Grimbridge's closed-down toy store located in?
    a. Sierra Madre   c. Inglewood
    b. Death Valley   d. Claremont

32. Who is the owner of the motel in Santa Mira, California where Dr. Challis and Ellie
Grimbridge rent a room?
    a. Ralphy   c. Rory
    b. Rourke   d. Rafferty

33. Why is Marge Guttman upset when she is first seen in the film?
    a. The factory overcharged her on her orders
    b. The factory lost her orders and has to reorder them for her
    c. The factory already mailed her the orders she had and she stayed in the motel for no reason
    d. The factory screwed up her orders and she has to stay in the motel again

34. What time is the town's curfew?
    a. 5:00 PM   c. 7:00 PM
    b. 6:00 PM   d. 8:00 PM

35. What did Starker say he would do to make sure that this'll be the last Halloween for Conal
Cochran and his factory?
    a. Blow it up with homemade bombs
    b. Burn it down with Molotov cocktails
    c. Demolish it with construction equipment
    d. Close them down by speaking with the Better Business Bureau

36. What did Teddy say was in the car that blew up when the android committed suicide?
    a. Plastic and Metal Shavings   c. Teeth and Bone Fragments
    b. Gasoline and Human Flesh   d. Blood and DNA

37. What color and type of car did Harry Grimbridge drive according to his daughter, Ellie?
    a. Blue Station Wagon   c. Red Station Wagon
    b. Orange Station Wagon   d. Green Station Wagon

38. What did Conal Cochran steal from Stonehenge and bring to the factory?
    a. Five-Ton Redstone   c. Five-Ton Bluestone
    b. Five-Ton Greenstone   d. Five-Ton Brimstone

39. What color was the blood in the androids when they become "deactivated"?
    a. Blue   c. Red
    b. Yellow   d. Orange

40. What type of mask was Little Buddy wearing when he and his family were killed?
    a. Skeleton   c. Frankenstein
    b. Jack-o'-Lantern   d. Witch

41. What venomous creature were Little Buddy's parents swarmed and killed by right after they witnessed the death of their son?
    a. Spiders   c. Snakes
    b. Scorpions   d. Bees

42. Which body part of Teddy's did the Silver Shamrock android drive the power drill through to kill her?
    a. Eye   c. Ear
    b. Mouth   d. Throat

43. What mask did Conal Cochran place over Dr. Challis' head when he kidnapped him?
    a. Witch   c. Jack-o'-Lantern
    b. Michael Myers   d. Skeleton

44. Conal Cochran said the last festival of Samhain took place how long ago?
    a. 2000 years ago   c. 5000 years ago
    b. 1000 years ago   d. 3000 years ago

45. What is the name of the marathon that the commercial will air to kill all the children watching while wearing their Silver Shamrock masks?
    a. Fear-a-Thon   c. Horror-a-Thon
    b. Scare-a-Thon   d. Scream-a-Thon

46. What are the last words of the film said by Dr. Challis?
    a. STOP IT!   c. QUIT IT!
    b. END IT!   d. RESET IT!

47. What did Harry Grimbridge say when he was brought to the hospital?
    a. They're going to find us. All of us.
    b. They're going to kill us. All of us.
    c. They're going to scare us. All of us.
    d. They're going to control us. All of us.

48. What horror movie was shown on the television in a commercial when Dr. Challis was at the bar?
    a. The Thing   c. Halloween
    b. The Texas Chainsaw Massacre   d. Psycho

49. What was Harry Grimbridge given a dosage of to calm him down?
    a. Thorazine   c. Risperidone
    b. Olanzapine   d. Quetiapine

50. What did the announcer say after the commercial sang eight more days till Halloween?
   a. Yes, kids, you, too can own one of the big Halloween three. That's right, three horrific masks to choose from. They're scary, they're terrifying, and they glow in the dark.
   b. Yes, kids, you, too can own one of the big Halloween three. That's right, three horrific masks to choose from. They're unique, they're iconic, and they glow in the dark.
   c. Yes, kids, you, too can own one of the big Halloween three. That's right, three horrific masks to choose from. They're fun, they're frightening, and they glow in the dark.
   d. Yes, kids, you, too can own one of the big Halloween three. That's right, three horrific masks to choose from. They're horrifying, they're monsterific, and they glow in the dark.

51. When driving to Santa Mira, Dr. Challis says you have to go how many miles after the next exit before turning right onto 33?
   a. Five   c. Ten
   b. Fifteen   d. Twenty

52. How many days till Halloween does the commercial say first?
   a. Eight   c. Nine
   b. Four   d. Seven

53. In the beginning of the film, where does it say they are currently located at?
   a. Northern California   c. Southern California
   b. Eastern California   d. Western California

54. In the opening credits, what Halloween-related object is being drawn?
   a. Ghost   c. Jack-o'-Lantern
   b. Witch   d. Black Cat

55. Where does Marge Guttman say her shop is located at?
   a. Union Square in San Diego
   b. Union Square in San Bernardino
   c. Union Square in San Jose
   d. Union Square in San Francisco

56. When did the receptionist at the Silver Shamrock Novelties headquarters say Harry Grimbridge picked up his order?
   a. October 20th   c. October 18th
   b. October 22nd   d. October 21st

57. After Ellie Grimbridge saw her father's car, who did Dr. Challis say it's time for?
   a. The Marines   c. The National Guard
   b. The Airforce   d. The S.W.A.T. Team

58. Who was Harry Grimbridge supposed to have dinner with on October 21st, someone who is involved with Michael Myers in a later sequel?
   a. Dr. Terrence Wynn   c. Minnie Blankenship
   b. Kara Strode   d. Jamie Lloyd

59. According to his records, where was Harry Grimbridge on October 19th?
    a. Football Game   c. Picking up Halloween Masks
    b. Merchant's Council Meeting   d. Dinner with Minnie Blankenship

60. According to Conal Cochran, who sold more Silver Shamrock masks than anyone else in the country?
    a. Marge Guttman   c. Buddy Kupfer
    b. Harry Grimbridge   d. Starker

61. What did Buddy Kupfer tell Dr. Challis that Conal Cochran invented as the ultimate practical joker?
    a. Sticky Toilet Paper   c. Whoopie Cushion
    b. Hand Buzzer   d. Fart Spray

62. What last name did Ellie Grimbridge say was hers and Dr. Challis'?
    a. Doe   c. Smith
    b. Jones   d. Anderson

63. The mask that Little Buddy wanted was turned down by Conal Cochran for what reason?
    a. It hasn't been through final processing
    b. It is another customer's order
    c. It hasn't been tested out yet
    d. It hasn't been logged for completion

64. What did Betty tell Ellie the way Conal Cochran became one of the richest men in the country was?
    a. By selling cheap gags and Halloween masks
    b. By selling practical jokes and toys
    c. By selling books he wrote
    d. By selling food and drinks

65. When visiting the factory, what made Dr. Challis suspicious?
    a. Seeing Harry Grimbridge's car
    b. Seeing two businessmen wearing suits in the parking lot
    c. Seeing Marge Guttman's corpse
    d. Seeing people being turned into androids

66. What are the cities on the commercial of children getting ready for the giveaway?
    a. St. Louis, Dallas, Philadelphia, Miami, Detroit, and Atlanta
    b. Boston, Phoenix, Sacramento, Pittsburgh, Baltimore, and Oklahoma City
    c. Dayton, New York City, Omaha, Baton Rouge, Los Angeles, and Seattle
    d. Chicago, Richmond, Houston, San Francisco, Las Vegas, and Minneapolis

67. What is the date when Dr. Challis asks Teddy to look into the businessman that killed Harry Grimbridge and then himself?
    a. Wednesday the 27th   c. Friday the 29th
    b. Saturday the 23rd   d. Saturday the 30th

68. Why does the sheriff think that the businessman killed Harry?
    a. Because he was on drugs   c. Because he was owed money
    b. Because he was a serial killer   d. Because he held a grudge

69. What is the name of the gas station in Santa Mira?
    a. Rafferty's Convenience Shop   c. Rafferty's Deluxe
    b. Rafferty's Gas Station   d. Rafferty's Pump

70. What does Rafferty tell Dr. Challis and Ellie why the motel is a good one to stay at?
    a. It's comfy, it's peaceful, and it's affordable
    b. It's cozy, it's quiet, and the price is right
    c. It's nice, it's warm, and the price is cheap
    d. It's beautiful, it's private, and it's free

71. What did Conal Cochran say happened to Marge Guttman?
    a. Misfire   c. Heart Attack
    b. Accidental Overdose   d. Stroke

72. What is Teddy's job title?
    a. Assistant Coroner   c. Coroner
    b. Forensic Expert   d. Tech Expert

73. In the beginning of the film, what is the date?
    a. October, Friday the 23rd
    b. October, Saturday the 23rd
    c. October, Sunday the 23rd
    d. October, Monday the 23rd

74. According to his records, where was Harry Grimbridge on October 18th?
    a. Picking up Halloween Masks   c. Dinner with Minnie Blankenship
    b. Football Game   d. Merchant's Council Meeting

75. What was seen recording Dr. Challis' conversation on the phone with Teddy?
    a. Tape Recorder   c. Bug
    b. Surveillance Camera   d. Camcorder

76. What did Dr. Challis' wife ask him when he called her from the factory?
    a. Is he stoned   c. Is he high
    b. Is he joking   d. Is he drunk

77. Who was the cinematographer of *Halloween 3: Season of the Witch*?
    a. Alan Howarth   c. Dean Cundey
    b. Millie Moore   d. Nigel Kneale

78. What nationality is Conal Cochran?
    a. Scottish   c. English
    b. Irish   d. American

79. When Dr. Challis was kidnapped, how did he escape?
    a. Through a ventilation shaft
    b. Killing an android and escaping through the door
    c. Pickpocketing a key from a visiting android and escaping through the door when the coast was clear
    d. Ellie came to his rescue

80. What did Dr. Challis decapitate Ellie with when he found out she was cloned into an android?
    a. Tire Iron   c. Machete
    b. Axe   d. Sickle

81. How many hours later did Harry Grimbridge arrive to the gas station where he collapsed?
    a. One Hour Later   c. Three Hours Later
    b. Two Hours Later   d. Four Hours Later

82. What documentary was Walter Jones watching in the gas station before Harry Grimbridge showed up?
    a. Stonehenge   c. Blood Moons
    b. Samhain   d. History of Haddonfield

83. What was Teddy researching that had her call the authorities right before she was murdered?
    a. Android parts from the car explosion
    b. Silver Shamrocks Halloween Mask
    c. Conal Cochran's plan for the commercial giveaway
    d. The history of the Silver Shamrocks factory

84. What was the name of the motel that Dr. Challis and Ellie stayed at?
    a. Silver Shamrocks Motel   c. Rose of Shannon Motel
    b. Irish n' Celtic Historical Motel   d. Samhain Monumental Motel

85. What did Conal Cochran say the hills ran red from at the last Samhain festival?
    a. From the blood of celebrants
    b. From the blood of sacrifices
    c. From the blood of criminals and the insane
    d. From the blood of children and animals

86. What is Stonehenge according to Conal Cochran?
    a. An ancient, ritualistic circle   c. An ancient, monumental circle
    b. An ancient, historical circle   d. An ancient, sacrificial circle

87. Who is the joke on according to Conal Cochran when speaking about the giveaway?
    a. The Children   c. The Halloween Celebrants
    b. The Country   d. The World

88. According to his records, what was Harry Grimbridge supposed to do on October 20th?
    a. File for bankruptcy   c. Go to the bank to receive his loan
    b. Pick up more Halloween masks   d. Order more inventory

89. What was the date that Harry Grimbridge checked into the motel?
    a. October 21st   c. October 20th
    b. October 18th   d. October 19th

90. What does Teddy say she's always good at?
    a. Romancing   c. Moonlighting
    b. Researching   d. Investigating

91. How many women are in the room clapping when Conal Cochran says Buddy Kupfer sold more Silver Shamrock masks than anyone else in the country?
    a. Five   c. Four
    b. Six   d. Eight

92. When Buddy wanted to see the final processing, what did Conal Cochran say that it involves that is very dangerous?
    a. Poisonous Chemicals   c. Radioactive Chemicals
    b. Acidic Chemicals   d. Volatile Chemicals

93. Where does Ellie say she lives?
    a. Sacramento   c. Los Angeles
    b. Oakland   d. Santa Monica

94. When arriving in Santa Mira, what small animal did Ellie say she felt like with Dr. Challis responding, "Company town"?
    a. Squirrel   c. Bug
    b. Goldfish   d. Spider

95. What kind of technology did Conal Cochran tell Dr. Challis he had in his underground laboratory?
    a. Ancient   c. Magical
    b. Dangerous   d. Advanced

96. How much money does Starker ask Dr. Challis if he could spare?
    a. $1.00   c. $5.00
    b. $10.00   d. $20.00

97. When Dr. Challis asks Teddy to look into Conal Cochran, what does Teddy say this'll cost Dr. Challis?
    a. Some serious vacation time   c. Some serious dinners
    b. Some serious overtime hours   d. Some serious raise discussions

98. What does the commercial announcer say to watch on the TV screen during the big giveaway?
    a. Magic Witch   c. Magic Pumpkin
    b. Magic Skeleton   d. Magic Cloverleaf

99. What kind of inspection did Conal Cochran say the final processing entails?
    a. Advanced   c. Quality
    b. Chemical   d. Security

100. When and where did Conal Cochran say the android of his grandmother was made?
    a. Munich, Germany in 1750   c. Munich, Germany in 1785
    b. Munich, Germany in 1880   d. Munich, Germany in 1825

Halloween 4: The Return of Michael Myers

1. Who was the final girl of *Halloween 4: The Return of Michael Myers*?
    a. Rachel Carruthers   c. Lindsay Wallace
    b. Jamie Lloyd   d. Kelly Meeker

2. What was the budget of *Halloween 4: The Return of Michael Myers*?
    a. $5,000,000   c. $10,000,000
    b. $7,000,000   d. $3,000,000

3. Who played Michael Myers?
    a. Dick Warlock   c. George P. Wilbur
    b. Don Shanks   d. Christopher Durand

4. When was *Halloween 4: The Return of Michael Myers* released into theaters?
    a. October 31, 1988   c. October 21, 1988
    b. October 25, 1988   d. October 28, 1988

5. What did *Halloween 4: The Return of Michael Myers* make at the box office?
    a. $17.5 million   c. $17.9 million
    b. $17.2 million   d. $17.7 million

6. Who directed *Halloween 4: The Return of Michael Myers*?
    a. John Carpenter   c. Tommy Lee Wallace
    b. Joe Chappelle   d. Dwight H. Little

7. Where did Sheriff Brackett move to after he retired from the Haddonfield police force?
    a. California   c. Hawaii
    b. Florida   d. North Carolina

8. How long has Michael Myers been in a coma for?
    a. Five Years   c. Eleven Years
    b. Ten Years   d. Seven Years

9. Who is Jamie Lloyd's mother?
    a. Darlene Carruthers   c. Laurie Strode
    b. Lindsay Wallace   d. Annie Brackett

10. What character from the first film has a small role in this film, but played by a different actor/actress?
    a. Tommy Doyle   c. Lindsay Wallace
    b. Laurie Strode   d. Sheriff Brackett

11. Who is the new sheriff of Haddonfield?
    a. Sheriff Ben Meeker   c. Sheriff Gary Hunt
    b. Sheriff Miguel Acosta   d. Sheriff Clark Hudson

12. Where did Reverend Jackson Sayer say he was going to?
    a. The Promise Land   c. Haddonfield
    b. Smith's Grove   d. Hollywood

13. Dr. Hoffman said if Dr. Loomis read what he'd be at Ridgemont?
    a. Notes   c. Emails
    b. Letters   d. Memos

14. Dr. Loomis seen six bodies between Haddonfield and what other town?
    a. Smith's Grove   c. Ridgemont
    b. Russellville   d. Blairstown

15. Which deputy was guarding the door at Sheriff Ben Meeker's house?
    a. Deputy Winslow   c. Deputy Logan
    b. Deputy Gary Hunt   d. Deputy Rick Cologne

16. When arguing with Brady, what nickname did Rachel give Kelly Meeker?
    a. Little Miss Hot Panties   c. Little Miss Hot Ass
    b. Little Miss Hot Breasts   d. Little Miss Hot Bra

17. What is the name of the power worker Michael killed?
    a. Braun   c. Barry
    b. Branson   d. Bucky

18. Who is the owner of the bar that leads the mob to find and kill Michael Myers?
    a. Unger   c. Big Al
    b. Earl   d. Orrin Gateway

19. Who went to ask Kelly out at the convenient store as a bet with Brady?
    a. Walter   c. Will
    b. Wade   d. Warren

20. What child actor was married to the lady who played the dead waitress?
    a. Corey Feldman   c. Shavar Ross
    b. Mike Lookinland   d. Gary Coleman

21. What was the name of the gas station that Michael Myers killed the mechanic and waitress
at?
    a. Penney's Gas Station   c. Pauley's Gas Station
    b. Polly's Gas Station   d. Perrey's Gas Station

22. Who are Jamie's foster parents?
    a. Richard and Darlene Carruthers   c. Ben and Kelly Meeker
    b. Brady and Rachel   d. Tommy and Lindsay

23. Who did Earl and his friends kill when they thought it was Michael Myers?
    a. Ted Hollister   c. Kyle
    b. Wade   d. Jackson Sayer

24. What town in Florida did Sheriff Brackett move to upon retirement?
    a. Orlando   c. St. Petersburg
    b. Miami   d. Fort Lauderdale

25. Where were Rachel's parents going to be at?
    a. The Waldorfs   c. The Fallbrooks
    b. The Shmenkmans   d. The Polygraphs

26. Where did Darlene say that Rachel's grandmother lives?
    a. Columbus   c. Cincinnati
    b. Cleveland   d. Parma

27. When is Jamie's bedtime?
    a. 9:00 PM   c. 10:00 PM
    b. 8:30 PM   d. 9:30 PM

28. What is the name of the convenient store that Brady works at?
    a. Discount Mart   c. Sale Mart
    b. BOGO Mart   d. Coupon Mart

29. What does Jamie stab her foster mother with, in a similar fashion to the way Michael stabbed his sister when he was a child?
    a. Butcher Knife   c. Glass Shard
    b. Knitting Needle   d. Scissors

30. What did Jamie dress as for Halloween?
    a. Fairy   c. Witch
    b. Clown   d. Princess

31. How long has Jackson Sayer been searching for Armageddon?
    a. Twenty-Five Years   c. Twenty Years
    b. Fifty Years   d. Thirty Years

32. Who played Jamie Lloyd?
    a. Leslie L. Rohland   c. Danielle Harris
    b. Kyle Richards   d. Stephanie Dees

33. What year did Sheriff Brackett retire?
    a. 1978   c. 1980
    b. 1979   d. 1981

34. Who did the special effects for Earl's death scene?
    a. Tom Savini   c. John Carpenter
    b. Sean S. Cunningham   d. John Carl Buechler

35. Where does Dr. Loomis take Jamie Lloyd to hide from Michael Myers?
    a. Jamie's House   c. The Myers' House
    b. The Schoolhouse   d. The Police Station

36. What did Dr. Hoffman say Dr. Loomis' position was?
    a. More Practical than Medical
    b. More Political than Medical
    c. More Ceremonial than Medical
    d. More Spiritual than Medical

37. What is the name of Rachel and Jamie's dog?
    a. Lester   c. Sundae
    b. Max   d. Mario

38. Who played Kelly Meeker?
    a. Ellie Cornell   c. Danielle Harris
    b. Kathleen Kinmont   d. Melody Gold

39. Who were the four men in the mob trying to find and kill Michael Myers?
    a. Earl, Big Al, Wade, and Orrin Gateway
    b. Earl, Big Al, Unger, and Orrin Gateway
    c. Earl, Big Al, Kyle, and Orrin Gateway
    d. Earl, Big Al, Brady, and Orrin Gateway

40. Who did the security guard at Ridgemont say has nothing to do with this place?
    a. God   c. Jesus
    b. Satan   d. Lucifer

41. Who was Brady and Wade hanging out with at the convenient store?
    a. Kyle   c. Tommy
    b. Earl   d. Bucky

42. Who played Brady?
    a. Beau Starr   c. Sasha Jenson
    b. Jeff Olson   d. Richard Stay

43. What achievement did Rachel ask Jamie if she was going for because she couldn't sleep?
    a. Eight-Year-Old Insomniacs Hall of Fame
    b. Nine-Year-Old Insomniacs Hall of Fame
    c. Six-Year-Old Insomniacs Hall of Fame
    d. Seven-Year-Old Insomniacs Hall of Fame

44. How many nights hasn't Jamie slept for?
    a. Five   c. Six
    b. Three   d. Four

45. What is the first name of Jamie's babysitter?
    a. Sharon   c. Susie
    b. Shannon   d. Stacy

46. Finish the quote that Rachel said to her mom: "Do you want a/an _________ for a daughter"?
    a. Mooer   c. Oinker
    b. Woofer   d. Meower

47. Since Jamie is too young to be Michael's legal guardian, who was then said to have been the owner of Michael's lifeless body?
    a. The State   c. Smith's Grove Sanitarium
    b. The Federal Prison   d. Dr. Loomis

48. How did Laurie Strode die?
    a. Michael Myers found and killed her
    b. She had cancer
    c. She was in a car accident
    d. She committed suicide

49. Who played Rachael Carruthers?
    a. Kathleen Kinmont   c. Karen Alston
    b. Ellie Cornell   d. Nancy Borgenicht

50. Who played the young Michael Myers when Jamie saw him in the convenient store's mirror?
    a. Will Sandin   c. Adam Gunn
    b. Erik Preston   d. Daeg Faerch

51. The character of Jamie Lloyd was named in homage to Jamie Lee Curtis. What was the original working first name of Jamie Lloyd in the script?
    a. Brittany   c. Barbie
    b. Billie   d. Bethany

52. Including the dog, what was the body count of the film?
    a. Eighteen   c. Nineteen
    b. Twenty   d. Sixteen

53. Which actress auditioned for the role of Jamie, but lost to Danielle Harris?
    a. Sara Gilbert   c. Kyle Richards
    b. Melissa Joan Hart   d. Jennifer Banko

54. Who was Jamie originally supposed to stab at the end of *Halloween 4: The Return of Michael Myers*?
    a. Lindsay Wallace
    b. Richard Carruthers
    c. Rachel Carruthers
    d. Sheriff Ben Meeker

55. Due to the death of Sundae in the movie, she makes how many dogs to die in the *Halloween* franchise?
    a. Four
    b. Three
    c. Two
    d. One

56. Which main cast member was supposed to die in a battle with Michael Myers?
    a. Dr. Sam Loomis
    b. Rachel Carruthers
    c. Jamie Lloyd
    d. Sheriff Ben Meeker

57. Due to budgetary constraints, which of the following scenes was eliminated from the film?
    a. The gas station explosion when Michael Myers sped off in the truck
    b. The ambulance accident that Michael Myers caused by killing the paramedics
    c. The house was supposed to catch fire when Rachel and Jamie ran from Michael Myers by climbing up the roof of the house
    d. Michael Myers being shot at by the firing squad and then blown up by a dynamite

58. This is the first film in the *Halloween* franchise that was wasn't involved with creatively?
    a. John Carpenter
    b. Moustapha Akkad
    c. Alan Howarth
    d. Alan B. McElroy

59. Which of the following films was the reason behind having Michael Myers return?
    a. Halloween 1 (1978)
    b. Halloween 2 (1981)
    c. Halloween 3: Season of the Witch
    d. Friday the 13th Part 6: Jason Lives

60. What is the tagline for *Halloween 4: The Return of Michael Myers*?
    a. Five Years Ago HE Changed the Face of Halloween. Tonight HE'S BACK!
    b. Seven Years Ago HE Changed the Face of Halloween. Tonight HE'S BACK!
    c. Ten Years Ago HE Changed the Face of Halloween. Tonight HE'S BACK!
    d. Twenty Years Ago HE Changed the Face of Halloween. Tonight HE'S BACK!

61. What did Reverend Jackson Sayer say you cannot kill?
    a. Evil
    b. The Devil
    c. Damnation
    d. End of the World

62. What did Earl say could land on Sheriff Ben Meeker's doorstep and all he'd do is spit once and get himself a shotgun?
    a. Aliens
    b. Demons
    c. Martians
    d. Giants

63. Dr. Hoffman said he hopes Dr. Loomis will do what with Michael Myers now gone?
    a. Transfer, Retire, or Move
    b. Transfer, Retire, or Die
    c. Transfer, Retire, or Quit
    d. Transfer, Retire, or Leave

64. How far is Haddonfield from the location the ambulance containing Michael Myers crashed?
    a. Two Hour Drive   c. Three Hour Drive
    b. Four Hour Drive   d. Five Hour Drive

65. What Caribbean island did Darlene tell Rachel would be a place they could go on vacation if Richard gets the promotion?
    a. The Bahamas   c. St. Lucia
    b. Cuba   d. Bermuda

66. What alarmed Earl and some of his loyal customers that something is wrong when they called the police station?
    a. The phone just kept ringing
    b. The phone went straight to an operator
    c. The phone was answered with no one talking on the other end
    d. The phone didn't ring

67. What kind of gun does Sheriff Meeker give to Brady to use for protection?
    a. Pistol   c. Rifle
    b. Shotgun   d. Assault Rifle

68. In the beginning of the film, what was the date shown?
    a. October 31, 1988   c. October 30, 1988
    b. October 27, 1988   d. October 29, 1988

69. What does the text say on Kelly Meeker's nightgown?
    a. Cops Do It By Their Own Rules
    b. Cops Do It By The Book
    c. Cops Do It By The Law
    d. Cops Do It By The Way They Were Trained

70. When Rachel goes with the kids to Sheriff Meeker's house, what Halloween monster was shown on the front door hanging as a decoration?
    a. Jack-o'-Lantern   c. Skeleton
    b. Witch   d. Vampire

71. How does Dr. Loomis know that Michael Myers was in Jamie's room at the Carruthers' house?
    a. Found a picture of Laurie Strode   c. Found Jamie's dog dead
    b. Found a message written in blood   d. Found the mask Michael wears

72. What two colors was the truck that Michael stole from the gas station?
    a. Orange and White
    b. Orange and Blue
    c. Orange and Black
    d. Orange and Red

73. What did Richard Carruthers dip his tie in by accident that he needed a new one?
    a. Orange Juice
    b. Tea
    c. Apple Juice
    d. Coffee

74. What was Darlene making for breakfast?
    a. Eggs
    b. French Toast
    c. Pancakes
    d. Cereal

75. Where did Darlene tell Richard another tie was at?
    a. Their Bedroom
    b. The Laundry Room
    c. The Living Room
    d. His Closet

76. Why can't Jamie's babysitter babysit?
    a. She broke her leg
    b. She broke her arm
    c. She broke her ankle
    d. She broke her foot

77. The kids that were teasing Jamie said her mommy is a what?
    a. Ghost
    b. Mummy
    c. Devil
    d. Demon

78. Who is Michael Myers to Jamie?
    a. Father
    b. Cousin
    c. Brother
    d. Uncle

79. When Jamie stabbed Darlene, what was Darlene doing for Jamie before she was stabbed?
    a. Running Jamie a bath
    b. Cooking Jamie dinner
    c. Making Jamie's bed
    d. Doing Jamie's laundry

80. How did Michael get to Sheriff Meeker's house?
    a. Followed Sheriff Meeker by walking there
    b. Hiding in the back of Deputy Logan's police car
    c. Drove there by following the state police cars
    d. Walked there after hearing about their whereabouts on the police scanner

81. How does Michael kill Brady?
    a. Impaled with a gun
    b. Neck crushed
    c. Shot with a gun
    d. Stabbed in the stomach

82. Why does Jamie attack and stab Darlene?
    a. Because of her relation to Michael Myers
    b. Because she hates her foster mom
    c. Because she misses her mom
    d. Because she witnessed murders

83. Who led the state police in the shooting of Michael Myers that supposedly killed him?
    a. Dr. Sam Loomis
    b. Sheriff Ben Meeker
    c. Deputy Logan
    d. The Lynch Mob

84. What branch of the military did Rachel say her parents most likely have the numbers for in case of an emergency?
    a. Army
    b. Airforce
    c. National Guard
    d. Marines

85. What did all the kids teasing Jamie keep repeating to her?
    a. Jamie's a killer
    b. Jamie's an orphan
    c. Jamie's a boogeyman
    d. Jamie's unwanted

86. What did Kelly Meeker make for Deputy Logan before her death?
    a. Tea
    b. Coffee
    c. Cider
    d. Hot Cocoa

87. What was Wade wearing in the convenient store?
    a. Halloween Mask
    b. Sunglasses
    c. Hat
    d. Headphones

88. How was Kelly Meeker killed by Michael?
    a. Throat was slit
    b. Strangled by Michael's bare hands
    c. Impaled with a gun
    d. Stabbed in the back

89. Where did Jamie's babysitter hurt herself at?
    a. School
    b. Ice Rink
    c. Cheerleading Practice
    d. Halloween Party

90. What did Darlene fall into when Jamie stabbed her?
    a. Closet
    b. Sink
    c. Bathtub
    d. Washing Machine

91. Finish the quote from Brady: _______ talks and ________ walks.
    a. Money talks and rejection walks
    b. Money talks and Kelly walks
    c. Money talks and bullshit walks
    d. Money talks and bravery walks

92. When this convertible of cheerleaders pulls over for Dr. Loomis, how many miles did the sign say to get to Haddonfield?
    a. 100 Miles
    b. 128 Miles
    c. 110 Miles
    d. 119 Miles

93. What were the lyrics of the song Reverend Jackson Sayer was singing in the truck with Dr. Loomis?
    a. Yes we'll gather at the river, the gorgeous, gorgeous river, gather with the saints at the river
    b. Yes we'll gather at the river, the holy, holy river, gather with the saints at the river
    c. Yes we'll gather at the river, the beautiful, beautiful river, gather with the saints at the river
    d. Yes we'll gather at the river, the marvelous, marvelous river, gather with the saints at the river

94. What time did Rachel say she'll be home from Trick or Treating with Jamie so Brady could stop by?
    a. 8:00 PM   c. 9:00 PM
    b. 7:00 PM   d. 10:00 PM

95. Who was the person on the first picture that Michael picked up in Jamie's room?
    a. Laurie Strode   c. Jamie Lloyd
    b. Himself as a child   d. Dr. Sam Loomis

96. Rachel found Brady cheating on her with who?
    a. Lindsay Wallace   c. Her Neighbor
    b. Kelly Meeker   d. Her mother

97. What did Michael Myers throw Dr. Loomis through when he was going after Jamie?
    a. The Schoolhouse Window   c. The Car Windshield
    b. The Sheriff's Front Door   d. The Police Car Windshield

98. Who of the lynch mob were killed and then had their corpses thrown off of the moving truck by Michael?
    a. Orrin Gateway, Unger, and Earl
    b. Orrin Gateway, Big Al, and Earl
    c. Big Al, Earl, and Unger
    d. Orrin Gateway, Big Al, and Unger

99. What was the mechanic asking for before he was killed by Michael?
    a. ¼ socket   c. ½ socket
    b. $^{1}/_{3}$ socket   d. $^{9}/_{16}$ socket

100. When the convertible of cheerleaders pulls over for Dr. Loomis, what are the names of the three towns/cities that are on the sign?
    a. Eaton, Haddonfield, and Smith's Grove
    b. Eaton, Haddonfield, and Russellville
    c. Eaton, Haddonfield, and Chicago
    d. Eaton, Haddonfield, and Ridgemont

Halloween 5: The Revenge of Michael Myers

1. Who played Michael Myers in *Halloween 5: The Revenge of Michael Myers*?
    a. Brad Loree
    b. Christopher Durand
    c. Tyler Mane
    d. Don Shanks

2. When was *Halloween 5: The Revenge of Michael Myers* released into theaters?
    a. October 31, 1989
    b. October 11, 1989
    c. October 29, 1989
    d. October 13, 1989

3. Who was the final girl of *Halloween 5: The Revenge of Michael Myers*?
    a. Rachel Carruthers
    b. Jamie Lloyd
    c. Tina Williams
    d. Samantha Thomas

4. What was revealed about the ending of *Halloween 4: The Return of Michael Myers* in this film?
    a. That Jamie Lloyd is the new Michael Myers
    b. That Darlene Carruthers has survived her attack from Jamie
    c. That Jamie Lloyd has been committed to Smith's Grove Sanitarium
    d. That Michael Myers is the father of Jamie Lloyd biologically

5. What is the body count of *Halloween 5: The Revenge of Michael Myers*, including Max and the opossum Dr. Loomis finds in the laundry chute?
    a. Nineteen
    b. Twenty-One
    c. Twenty
    d. Seventeen

6. What was the name of Rachel's dog?
    a. Sundae
    b. Lester
    c. Max
    d. Gordon

7. How many police officers were killed in the shootout at the police station by the man in black?
    a. Eight
    b. Ten
    c. Nine
    d. Five

8. What did Michael use to slice Samantha's stomach opened?
    a. Sickle
    b. Hatchet
    c. Scythe
    d. Butcher Knife

9. How many years have passed since Michael's supposed death to his alleged resurrection?
    a. Two Years
    b. Three Years
    c. One Year
    d. Five Years

10. What was the budget of *Halloween 5: The Revenge of Michael Myers*?
    a. $3,000,000
    b. $2,000,000
    c. $4,000,000
    d. $5,000,000

11. What pet did the Mountain Man have?
    a. Spider
    b. Mouse
    c. Snake
    d. Parrot

12. How did Michael survive the TNT blast after being shoot by a firing squad?
    a. He shielded himself with a huge boulder
    b. He wasn't near the TNT blast
    c. He disappeared from the area and his body wasn't in the hole
    d. He escaped through a hole in the ground and floated down the river

13. What weapon does Michael kill Rachel with?
    a. Butcher Knife
    b. Scissors
    c. Glass Shard
    d. Hunting Knife

14. What animal does Spitz and Samantha see in the barn?
    a. Puppy
    b. Kitten
    c. Rabbit
    d. Mouse

15. What was the name of Jamie's doctor at the clinic?
    a. Dr. Miguel Hart
    b. Dr. Max Hart
    c. Dr. Mickey Hart
    d. Dr. Mark Hart

16. Who directed *Halloween 5: The Revenge of Michael Myers*?
    a. Rick Rosenthal
    b. Dominique Othenin-Girard
    c. Steve Miner
    d. Dwight H. Little

17. What did *Halloween 5: The Revenge of Michael Myers* make at the box office?
    a. $11.6 million
    b. $11.9 million
    c. $11.5 million
    d. $11.1 million

18. Which of the following characters from *Halloween 4: The Return of Michael Myers* doesn't return in this film?
    a. Sheriff Ben Meeker
    b. Rachel Carruthers
    c. Lindsay Wallace
    d. Jamie Lloyd

19. What was the hole that Michael Myers fell down after being shot by a firing squad?
    a. Fox Hole
    b. Grave
    c. Mine Shaft
    d. Sand Trap

20. How does Jamie know when Michael will kill someone?
    a. She has some type of telepathic link to Michael
    b. She has the heart of a killer
    c. She heard the voice Michael did when he was a kid
    d. She has genetic connections to him and his killer instincts

21. What is Jamie's condition at the clinic?
    a. She has been rendered mentally and psychologically insane
    b. She has been rendered physical and emotionally unstable
    c. She has been rendered a mute due to psychological trauma
    d. She has been rendered verbally, visually, and mentally crazy

22. What is Tina's boyfriend's name?
    a. Mikey   c. Jason
    b. Freddy   d. Chucky

23. What did Billy dress up as for Halloween?
    a. Vampire   c. Pirate
    b. Clown   d. Mummy

24. After Dr. Loomis attacked Michael and trapped him, why does he collapse?
    a. He has a heart attack
    b. He is suffering from exhaustion
    c. He has a stroke
    d. He is relieved on Michael's capture

25. Who's corpses does Jamie see in the attic of the Myers house?
    a. Rachel Carruthers, Spitz, and Max
    b. Rachel Carruthers, Samantha Thomas, and Max
    c. Rachel Carruthers, Mikey, and Max
    d. Rachel Carruthers, Tina Williams, and Max

26. What was the name of the gas station that Tina was at when Jamie felt the presence of Michael Myers?
    a. Dick's Gas Station   c. Darren's Gas Station
    b. Denny's Gas Station   d. Dale's Gas Station

27. What was the name of the Mountain Man's parrot?
    a. Cookie   c. Snookie
    b. Pookie   d. Rookie

28. Who was the name of Jamie's nurse at the clinic?
    a. Nurse Peggy   c. Nurse Penny
    b. Nurse Patsey   d. Nurse Perrey

29. What did Jamie dress up as for Halloween?
    a. Clown   c. Witch
    b. Fairy   d. Princess

30. What was the name of the store that Rachel and Tina went to?
    a. Quick Food Mart   c. Discount Mart
    b. Convenient Service Mart   d. Cheap Item Mart

31. What did the note say that was thrown through the window?
    a. The Evil Child Is The Boogeyman
    b. The Evil Child Must Die
    c. The Evil Child Must Be Sacrificed
    d. The Evil Child Is What He Wants

32. What was the location of the big Halloween party that Tina was going to?
    a. Cornmaze Farm   c. Tower Farm
    b. Pumpkin Farm   d. Raver Farm

33. What did Jamie write on her chalkboard?
    a. He's Still Alive   c. He's Coming For Me
    b. He's In Haddonfield   d. He's Gonna Sacrifice Me

34. What did the officer say the location of the gas station was?
    a. 5th and Main   c. 1st and Main
    b. 2nd and Main   d. 3rd and Main

35. Where was Jamie Lloyd stabbed originally, but it was cut from the film due to the MPAA deeming it as "too disturbing"?
    a. Leg   c. Arm
    b. Foot   d. Hand

36. When Rachel visits Jamie, as she is leaving, how long did she tell Jamie on when she'll be back?
    a. One Day   c. Three Days
    b. Two Days   d. One Week

37. When Jamie couldn't breathe, what did Dr. Max Hart say he had to open for Jamie so she won't die?
    a. Esophagus   c. Trachea
    b. Heart   d. Lungs

38. How many cases of alcohol can Spitz get for Mikey from the store he works at?
    a. Two Cases   c. Four Cases
    b. Three Cases   d. Five Cases

39. What is the name of Spitz's boss?
    a. Mr. Casy   c. Mr. Cosick
    b. Mr. Collins   d. Mr. Cruz

40. How old is Jamie Lloyd?
    a. Ten Years Old   c. Eight Years Old
    b. Nine Years Old   d. Seven Years Old

41. Who was dressed up as Michael Myers as a prank at the Halloween party?
    a. Mikey   c. Tina Williams
    b. Samantha Thomas   d. Spitz

42. What does Tina want to get at the gas station?
    a. Lottery Tickets   c. Case of Beer
    b. Change for a $20   d. Pack of Cigarettes

43. While waiting for Michael Myers in the Myers house, what is Jamie doing in the bedroom?
    a. Setting traps   c. Pacing back and forth
    b. Brushing her hair   d. Crying

44. *Halloween 5: The Revenge of Michael Myers* is the only movie in the *Halloween* franchise to never be released in which European country?
    a. United Kingdom   c. Italy
    b. France   d. Germany

45. How many dogs have been killed in the *Halloween* franchise, including Max?
    a. Three   c. Four
    b. Five   d. Six

46. What popped out dead in the laundry chute when Dr. Loomis was snooping around the Myers house?
    a. Opossum   c. Skunk
    b. Cat   d. Rat

47. What unique weapon does Michael use on Mikey?
    a. Garden Claw   c. Hoe
    b. Rake   d. Shovel

48. Whose bodies does Tina Williams have fallen on her when she is in the barn?
    a. Spitz and Rachel Carruthers
    b. Spitz and Mikey
    c. Spitz and Samantha Thomas
    d. Deputy Nick Ross and Deputy Tom Farrah

49. Who was the officer that was watching Jamie at the end of the film after Michael was taken to the station?
    a. Sheriff Ben Meeker   c. Deputy Tony
    b. Deputy Charlie Bloch   d. Deputy Eddy Grey

50. How did Michael Myers kill the Mountain Man?
    a. Slit his throat   c. Knifed in the back
    b. Strangled with Michael's bare hands   d. Head bashed on a rock wall

51. When was Spitz killed by Michael with a pitchfork?
    a. When looking for Samantha in the barn
    b. When yelling for help after finding a dead body
    c. When having sex with Samantha in the barn
    d. When he found a cat with blood on its fur

52. What does Rachel's death scene resemble?
    a. The time that Michael killed his sister when he was a boy
    b. The time that Jamie Lloyd stabbed her foster mother
    c. The time that Dr. Loomis put Michael in a coma for ten years
    d. The time that Rachel stopped Michael exactly one-year prior

53. Who played the role of Samantha Thomas?
    a. Ellie Cornell   c. Danielle Harris
    b. Tamara Glynn   d. Wendi Kaplan

54. How many different sections of the laundry chute were filmed during the laundry chute scene?
    a. Ten   c. Thirty
    b. Twenty   d. Fifty

55. Which musician was the Man in Black's wardrobe made to resemble?
    a. Tommy Lee Jones   c. Alice Cooper
    b. Elvis Presley   d. Johnny Cash

56. When Michael was wearing a different mask while pretending to be Tina's boyfriend, Mikey, it was originally scripted that he wore a mask of which United States president's face until it was changed due to not involving the film with politics?
    a. Abraham Lincoln   c. George H.W. Bush
    b. Ronald Reagan   d. Jimmy Carter

57. What is the tagline of *Halloween 5: The Revenge of Michael Myers*?
    a. Michael Lives. And This Time They're Prepared
    b. Michael Lives. And This Time They're Aware
    c. Michael Lives. And This Time They're Ready
    d. Michael Lives. And This Time They're Ending It

58. Who created the music for *Halloween 5: The Revenge of Michael Myers*?
    a. John Carpenter   c. Alan Howarth
    b. Harry Manfredini   d. Malek Akkad

59. Who was in charge of cinematography on set for *Halloween 5: The Revenge of Michael Myers*?
    a. Robert Draper   c. Dean Cundey
    b. Peter Lyons Collister   d. David Geddes

60. Who played the role of Spitz?
    a. Matthew Walker
    b. Jeffrey Landman
    c. Troy Evans
    d. Beau Starr

61. How is Tina classified as the hero of the film?
    a. She killed Michael Myers
    b. She found out how Michael Myers can be stopped
    c. She sacrificed herself to save Jamie's life
    d. She knows why Michael kills on Halloween nights

62. Where did Sheriff Ben Meeker take Michael at the end of the film so he can spend the rest of his days there until he was broken out by the Man in Black?
    a. Police Station Holding Cell
    b. Solitary Confinement
    c. Maximum Security Prison
    d. Psychiatric Ward

63. What type of explosive do the state troopers throw down the mine shaft to kill Michael once and for all at the beginning of the film?
    a. Grenade
    b. Dynamite
    c. TNT
    d. Bomb

64. Who played the role of Mikey?
    a. Frank Como
    b. Matthew Walker
    c. David Ursin
    d. Jonathan Chapin

65. Who does Michael Myers kill at the clinic?
    a. Billy
    b. Nurse Patsey
    c. Dr. Max Hart
    d. Both B and C

66. Where does Michael kill Tina's boyfriend, Mikey?
    a. At the Halloween party
    b. In his car
    c. In a car garage
    d. In a barn

67. How does the film begin?
    a. With Michael floating down the river
    b. With the ending of the previous film
    c. With Michael being found by a Mountain Man
    d. With Rachel visiting Jamie at the clinic

68. The script included a "clown theme" of the bumbling cops, Deputies Nick Ross and Tom Farrah, to pay homage to which classic film?
    a. IT
    b. The Funhouse
    c. The Last House on the Left
    d. Friday the 13th

69. Who played the role of Tina Williams?
    a. Tamara Glynn
    b. Danielle Harris
    c. Wendi Kaplan
    d. Ellie Cornell

70. The Mountain Man in the beginning of the film was originally going to be what?
    a. A young man by the name of Dr. Evil
    b. A young man by the name of Dr. Shape
    c. A young man by the name of Dr. Death
    d. A young man by the name of Dr. Blood

71. How was Rachel originally going to be killed?
    a. Being stabbed in the eye with a pair of scissors
    b. Having her head chopped off with a butcher knife
    c. Having her body chopped into pieces with a butcher knife
    d. Having a pair of scissors shoved down her throat

72. What plot point of the film did Donald Pleasence have disagreements about with Moustapha Akkad and the director?
    a. Donald thought that Jamie should be "all-evil"
    b. Donald thought that Rachel should not have been killed
    c. Donald thought that there should've been more blood and gore
    d. Donald thought that Dr. Sam Loomis should've been killed off

73. What state was *Halloween 5: The Revenge of Michael Myers* filmed in?
    a. California   c. Arizona
    b. Louisiana   d. Utah

74. Who played the role of Billy?
    a. Corey Feldman   c. Troy Evans
    b. Harper Roisman   d. Jeffrey Landman

75. What did Michael Myers use to kill Deputies Nick Ross and Tom Farrah?
    a. Scythe   c. Machete
    b. Butcher Knife   d. Pitchfork

76. When Michael lifted his mask, what did Jamie do that made him go psycho?
    a. She went to give him a hug
    b. She went to wipe his tears from his eyes
    c. She went to give him a kiss
    d. She went to take the knife off of him

77. Originally, what was going to be in the shack of the young man that he would've used to bring Michael back to life, but was cut in favor of the Mountain Man?
    a. Ancient Runes and Crystals
    b. Ancient Runes and Potions
    c. Ancient Runes and Tablets
    d. Ancient Runes and Spells

78. What was the address of where the Myers house was filmed?
    a. 1005 1st Avenue   c. 1007 1st Avenue
    b. 1009 1st Avenue   d. 1134 1st Avenue

79. How did Dr. Loomis weaken Michael?
    a. Shot him six times with his gun
    b. Beat him with a wooden plank
    c. Shot him with a tranquilizer gun
    d. He strapped him into a strait jacket

80. How did Dr. Loomis lure Michael into his trap to drop the net onto him?
    a. He kept baiting Michael with insulting words
    b. He had Michael chase him
    c. He used Jamie as bait to lure Michael
    d. He recreated the scene of the night he killed his sister

81. What disability does Billy have?
    a. Autism   c. Tourette's Syndrome
    b. Bipolar   d. Stuttering

82. What happens to Jamie during the pageant?
    a. She falls off the stage when getting another telekinetic vision of Michael
    b. She starts talking and warning everyone of Michael
    c. She runs off the stage to look for Rachel and Tina
    d. She starts hyperventilating when reliving what she did to her foster mother

83. When Spitz and Samantha are making love, what "goof" happens during the sex scene?
    a. The condom Spitz has is opened
    b. Samantha takes her gloves off twice
    c. Spitz and Samantha are obviously wearing clothes while making love
    d. You can see the shadow of the director

84. What happens to Sheriff Ben Meeker at the end of the film?
    a. He dies in the shootout of the police station
    b. He takes Jamie to protection from the police station shootout
    c. He, along with Jamie, find Michael gone after the police station shootout
    d. He takes Dr. Loomis to visit Michael in the jail cell only to find out he escaped

85. What kind of dog is Max?
    a. Labrador Retriever   c. German Shepard
    b. Doberman   d. Rottweiler

86. Where did Dr. Loomis pray Michael would go but realized would not have him?
    a. Smith's Grove Sanitarium   c. Hell
    b. Death's Door   d. The Afterlife

87. What is the name of the store that Spitz works at?
    a. Victor Drug Store   c. Val Drug Store
    b. Vincent Drug Store   d. Vito Drug Store

88. Which character from the *Friday the 13th* franchise does Jamie Lloyd have a striking parallel with?
    a. Reggie the Reckless   c. Tina Shepard
    b. Tommy Jarvis   d. Rennie Wickham

89. What was Samantha dressed as at the Halloween party?
    a. Angel   c. Witch
    b. Devil   d. French Maid

90. What personality trait does Tina have?
    a. Outgoing   c. Mischievous
    b. Prankster   d. Obnoxious

91. What does Jamie hide in when running from Michael and after she finds the bodies in his attic?
    a. Casket   c. Bathtub
    b. Closet   d. Laundry Chute

92. All the other actors who played Michael Myers were 6'2" except for Don Shanks who was how tall?
    a. 6'1"   c. 6'0"
    b. 5'10"   d. 6'3"

93. The working title of *Halloween 5: The Revenge of Michael Myers* was what?
    a. Halloween 5: The Wrath of Michael Myers
    b. Halloween 5: Season of Evil
    c. Halloween 5: And Things Go Pump in the Night
    d. Halloween 5: Day of the Dead

94. How many minutes does Rachel appear in *Halloween 5: The Revenge of Michael Myers*?
    a. 30 Minutes   c. 15 Minutes
    b. 25 Minutes   d. 20 Minutes

95. What did Dr. Loomis repeatedly hit Michael with?
    a. Lead Pipe   c. 2x4
    b. Hammer   d. His fists

96. Why was Rachel's death scene changed from the original death written in the script?
    a. Because the actress who played Rachel wanted a more gruesome death scene
    b. Because the actress who played Rachel thought the death was too gruesome
    c. Because the actress who played Rachel originally wanted to survive the film
    d. Because the actress who played Rachel didn't want a child actress to see such a death

97. What did Moustapha Akkad say one of his biggest regrets was in this movie?
    a. That he killed off Rachel Carruthers
    b. That Dr. Sam Loomis wasn't killed off
    c. That the ending wasn't originally written
    d. That the Man in Black wasn't revealed

98. What magazine was the director quoted as saying that the ending of the film wasn't scripted?
    a. Fangoria Magazine   c. Apex Magazine
    b. Rue Morgue Magazine   d. Nightmare Magazine

99. Which scene with Billy was originally cut from the film to avoid an X rating with the MPAA?
    a. Being killed by Michael Myers
    b. Being attacked by Michael Myers
    c. Being chased by Michael Myers
    d. Being hit in the leg with the car Michael Myers was driving

100. This is the last film of the series to feature what in the opening credits?
    a. The Halloween theme song
    b. Having the names of the cast
    c. Having a pumpkin graphic
    d. Having the title of the film featured

Halloween: The Curse of Michael Myers

1. When was *Halloween: The Curse of Michael Myers* released into theaters?
   a. September 29, 1995
   b. September 30, 1995
   c. September 25, 1995
   d. September 18, 1995

2. What was the budget of *Halloween: The Curse of Michael Myers*?
   a. $3,000,000
   b. $7,000,000
   c. $5,000,000
   d. $9,000,000

3. Danielle Harris refused to return as Jamie Lloyd. Who took over the role of Jamie Lloyd?
   a. Jennifer Banko
   b. Kyle Richards
   c. J.C. Brandy
   d. Amber Pawlick

4. Who directed *Halloween: The Curse of Michael Myers*?
   a. Dwight H. Little
   b. Joe Chappelle
   c. John Carpenter
   d. Tommy Lee Wallace

5. Which character from the original Halloween returned as a main character?
   a. Laurie Strode
   b. Lindsay Wallace
   c. Tommy Doyle
   d. Sheriff Brackett

6. What is the curse that keeps driving Michael Myers to kill?
   a. Bonfire
   b. Skull
   c. Thorn
   d. Hellfire

7. Who was the final girl of *Halloween: The Curse of Michael Myers*?
   a. Debra Strode
   b. Jamie Lloyd
   c. Kara Strode
   d. Beth

8. Who played Michael Myers?
   a. Nick Castle
   b. George P. Wilbur
   c. Dick Warlock
   d. Don Shanks

9. What happened to Dr. Loomis?
   a. He died
   b. He is institutionalized
   c. He moved to Russellville
   d. He is retired

10. What movie was Mrs. Blankenship watching in her home?
    a. The Phantom of the Opera
    b. Citizen Kane
    c. The Wizard of Oz
    d. Casablanca

11. What was the body count of *Halloween: The Curse of Michael Myers*?
    a. Twenty
    b. Twenty-One
    c. Twenty-Two
    d. Twenty-Three

12. What did *Halloween: The Curse of Michael Myers* make in the box office?
    a. $15.5 million   c. $15.3 million
    b. $15.7 million   d. $15.1 million

13. Which actress was considered for and later turned down for the role of Beth?
    a. Leah Remini   c. Candace Cameron-Bure
    b. Denise Richards   d. Julia Roberts

14. What was the original working title of *Halloween: The Curse of Michael Myers*?
    a. Halloween 666: The Curse of Michael Myers
    b. Halloween 666: The History of Michael Myers
    c. Halloween 666: The Origin of Michael Myers
    d. Halloween 666: The Lore of Michael Myers

15. When Danielle Harris turned down the film, it was because Dimension Films refused to pay her how much money for the role?
    a. $10,000   c. $7,000
    b. $5,000   d. $3,000

16. What name did Tommy give to Jamie's baby?
    a. Stephen   c. Scott
    b. Sean   d. Stanley

17. Which character hears the voice that Michael once heard as a child?
    a. Danny Strode   c. Tommy Doyle
    b. Tim Strode   d. Jamie Lloyd

18. Who was revealed as being the Man in Black from *Halloween 5: The Revenge of Michael Myers* who ultimately helped Michael escape from the maximum security prison?
    a. Dr. Sam Loomis   c. Tommy Doyle
    b. John Strode   d. Dr. Terrence Wynn

19. What room number in Smith's Grove Sanitarium is Kara being locked in?
    a. 233   c. 235
    b. 237   d. 239

20. What character from *Halloween: The Curse of Michael Myers* was named after Bob Simms from *Halloween (1978)*?
    a. Barry Simms   c. Bobby Simms
    b. Billy Simms   d. Barney Simms

21. What type of truck was Jamie driving in the beginning of the film?
    a. Chevrolet Colorado   c. Chevrolet Silverado
    b. Chevrolet Tahoe   d. Chevrolet Blazer

22. What did Tim's t-shirt say?
    a. Barry Kicks Ass
    b. Barry Slaps Ass
    c. Barry Kisses Ass
    d. Barry Kills Ass

23. What was Beth dressed as for the Halloween party?
    a. Witch
    b. Queen
    c. Bride of Frankenstein
    d. Princess

24. What did the voice tell Michael to do when he was a child, according to Mrs. Blankenship?
    a. To hate his family
    b. To kill his family
    c. To become evil
    d. To leave his family

25. Besides Tommy and Dr. Loomis, who else knew of Jamie's baby?
    a. Mrs. Blankenship
    b. Dr. Terrence Wynn
    c. John Strode
    d. Debra Strode

26. What was the phone number to Barry Simms' station?
    a. 1-800-968-7836 (YOU SUCK)
    b. 1-800-968-7814 (YOU SUCK)
    c. 1-800-968-7825 (YOU SUCK)
    d. 1-800-968-7837 (YOU SUCK)

27. What did Danny dress up as for Halloween?
    a. The identical twin brother of Tim Strode
    b. The identical twin brother of Tommy Doyle
    c. The identical twin brother of Michael Myers
    d. The identical twin brother of Barry Simms

28. How did Mrs. Blankenship know Michael Myers?
    a. She adopted him after he killed his sister
    b. She visited him during her volunteer work at Smith's Grove Sanitarium
    c. She helped him plot his revenge on Haddonfield in 1978
    d. She babysat him the night he killed his sister

29. What does it say on the sign that was posted on the Strode's front lawn?
    a. He's Back
    b. He's Alive
    c. He's Here
    d. He's Coming

30. What was the name of Barry Simms' radio show?
    a. Smacktalk with Barry Simms
    b. Haddonfield Gossip with Barry Simms
    c. Sex Therapy with Barry Simms
    d. Backtalk with Barry Simms

31. What color and make vehicle did Tommy have?
    a. Red Blazer   c. Red Ferrari
    b. Red Mercedes   d. Red Jeep

32. What was the name of the nurse that helped Jamie escape?
    a. Marcia   c. Megan
    b. Mary   d. Margaret

33. What was Mrs. Blankenship's first name, as told of in *Halloween 3: Season of the Witch*?
    a. Mary Ann   c. Mary Ellen
    b. Maxine   d. Minnie

34. What colors was the truck that Jamie was driving in the beginning of the film?
    a. Blue and White   c. Blue and Red
    b. Black and White   d. Black and Blue

35. Who played the role of Tommy Doyle?
    a. Paul Rudd   c. Brian Andrews
    b. Thom Mathews   d. John Shepherd

36. Who's house did Beth tell Barry Simms on his show that Tim's family lives in?
    a. The Doyle House   c. The Myers House
    b. The Wallace House   d. The Meeker House

37. What was Tim dressed as for the Halloween party?
    a. Dracula   c. Wolfman
    b. Frankenstein   d. Mad Scientist

38. What did Barry Simms ask Tim if Beth does in bed?
    a. If Beth wears crotchless panties and fakes her orgasms
    b. If Beth wears crotchless panties and curses uncontrollably
    c. If Beth wears crotchless panties and barks like a dog
    d. If Beth wears crotchless panties and roleplays

39. Who is John and Debra's niece?
    a. Jamie Lloyd   c. Kara Strode
    b. Laurie Strode   d. Rachel Carruthers

40. What was Kara studying for at her college?
    a. Sociology   c. Biology
    b. Psychology   d. Physiology

41. Which of the following is one of the differences in the producer's cut that was excluded from the theater release of the film?
    a. Danny hears the voice Michael heard as a child   c. Jamie's death scene
    b. The ending of the film   d. All of the Above

42. What did the little girl say when she was under the tree that Barry Simms' corpse was located?
    a. Mommy it's a man   c. Mommy it's raining red
    b. Mommy it's warm raindrops   d. Mommy it's a climber

43. Who played the role of Kara Strode?
    a. J.C. Brandy   c. Marianne Hagan
    b. Kim Darby   d. Mariah O'Brien

44. Why does Dr. Wynn visit Dr. Loomis?
    a. Because he wants Dr. Loomis to find Michael Myers
    b. Because he wants Dr. Loomis to come out of retirement and return to Smith's Grove
    c. Because he wants Dr. Loomis to study the reason Michael kills on Halloween
    d. Because he wants Dr. Loomis to join his cult

45. When does Michael Myers know to kill on Halloween?
    a. When the constellations form the symbol of the jack-o'-lantern
    b. When the constellations form the symbol of the devil
    c. When the constellations form the symbol of the thorn
    d. When the constellations form the symbol of the Celtics

46. According to the Producer's Cut of *Halloween: The Curse of Michael Myers*, who is the father of Jamie's baby?
    a. Tommy Doyle   c. Michael Myers
    b. Tim Strode   d. Dr. Terrence Wynn

47. Who played the role of Danny Strode?
    a. Paul Rudd   c. Devin Gardner
    b. Keith Bogart   d. Leo Geter

48. Who were the characters of John and Debra Strode named after?
    a. John Wayne and Debra Jo Rupp   c. John Lennon and Debra Messing
    b. John Carpenter and Debra Hill   d. John Travolta and Debra Marshall

49. Who turned down the role of Barry Simms when he was offered the role?
    a. Alice Cooper   c. Bubba the Love Sponge
    b. Marilyn Manson   d. Howard Stern

50. How many different drafts did the film go through?
    a. Ten   c. Twelve
    b. Eleven   d. Thirteen

51. Why did Marianne Hagan almost not get the role of Kara Strode?
    a. Because Miramax Films thought she was too thin and her chin was too pointy
    b. Because Miramax Films thought she was too old and too boring
    c. Because Miramax Films thought she was too ugly and too feminine
    d. Because Miramax Films thought she was too unbelievable and too bad of an actress

52. In January 1995, *Entertainment Tonight* had a special on making this movie where it stated that it was going to be called what in early stages of development?
    a. Halloween 6: Michael's Return
    b. Halloween 6: Michael's Curse
    c. Halloween 6: Michael's Back
    d. Halloween 6: Michael's Revenge

53. After Michael killed his entire family in his bloodline due to the Curse of Thorn, what would happen then?
    a. The curse would allow Michael to be killed
    b. The curse would be passed onto another young child
    c. The curse would cease to exist
    d. The curse would make Michael Myers disappear from existence

54. Where does the Curse of Thorn come from?
    a. Ancient Celtic Rituals   c. Ancient Irish Rituals
    b. Ancient Samhain Rituals   d. Ancient Wiccan Rituals

55. In *Halloween (1978)*, Dr. Wynn makes a brief appearance saying Michael cannot drive a car. What does Dr. Wynn say in *Halloween: The Curse of Michael Myers* on how Michael learned to drive a car?
    a. He allowed him to take driving lessons at a local DMV
    b. He taught him how to drive a car
    c. He blackmailed Marion Chambers into teaching him how to drive a car
    d. He allowed Michael to teach himself how to drive a car around the parking lot of Smith's Grove Sanitarium

56. What is Dr. Wynn's position at Smith's Grove Sanitarium?
    a. Chief Psychiatrist   c. Chief Executive Officer
    b. Chief Administrator   d. Chief Operating Officer

57. What did Beth say Tommy rates on a weirdness scale of 1 to 10?
    a. Eleven   c. Thirteen
    b. Twelve   d. Twenty

58. Who played the role of Dr. Terrence Wynn?
    a. Mitchell Ryan   c. Donald Pleasence
    b. Bradford English   d. Keith Bogart

59. What was said during the opening narration of the film?
   a. After my stroke six years ago they practically had to hold a pistol to my head to get me to retire. But things are different now- I'm different. I've buried the ghosts; I've buried them in this manuscript. I don't want to practice medicine anymore.
   b. I've wanted to believe it. But I've felt Michael's presence, behind these walls, just like all those years ago. Plotting, staring, Staring. Waiting for some signal. I can't go through this again, not alone. Please, as my colleague, as my friend. Help me.
   c. After Jamie escape last night, I knew she would come to you. And I knew you would lead us to her baby, her very special baby. I needed her, just as I need you now. It's your destiny Sam, it lives inside you. It always has, you know that don't you?
   d. When Michael Myers was six years old, he stabbed his sister to death. He was locked up for years in Smith's Grove Sanitarium, but he escaped. Soon after, Halloween became another word for mayhem! One by one, he killed his entire family, until his nine-year-old niece, Jamie Lloyd, was the only one left alive. Six years ago - Halloween night - Michael and Jamie vanished. Most people believed them dead but I believe someone hid them away. Someone who keeps Michael, protects him... tries to control him. If there's one thing I know, you can't control evil. You can lock it up, burn it, and bury it, and pray that it dies, but it never will. It just... rests awhile. You can lock your doors, and say your prayers, but the evil is out there... waiting. And maybe, just maybe... it's closer than you think!

60. What was the story Mrs. Blankenship told Danny?
   a. Spirits and powers of the flame, attend and witness this ritual. Bear our gifts to Thorn. Open us to the path of Darkness. By these runes transform us. Let the hammer descend upon the Chosen One to whom we offer this sacrifice of Innocent Blood. And then Danny, your journey begins. Kill for him!
   b. When Michael Myers was six years old, he stabbed his sister to death. He was locked up for years in Smith's Grove Sanitarium, but he escaped. Soon after, Halloween became another word for mayhem! One by one, he killed his entire family, until his nine-year-old niece, Jamie Lloyd, was the only one left alive. Six years ago - Halloween night - Michael and Jamie vanished. Most people believed them dead but I believe someone hid them away. Someone who keeps Michael, protects him... tries to control him. If there's one thing I know, you can't control evil. You can lock it up, burn it, and bury it, and pray that it dies, but it never will. It just... rests awhile. You can lock your doors, and say your prayers, but the evil is out there... waiting. And maybe, just maybe... it's closer than you think!
   c. A long, long time ago, it was a night of great power. When the days grew short, the spirits of the dead, returned to their homes to warm themselves by the fire's side. All across the land, huge bonfires were lit. Ohhh, there was a marvelous celebration. People danced, and they played games, and they dressed up in costumes, hoping to ward off the evil spirits. Especially the boogey man.
   d. b. In order to appease the gods, the Druid priests held fire rituals. Prisoners of war, criminals, the insane, animals... were... burned alive in baskets. By observing the way they died, the Druids believed they could see omens of the future. Two thousand years later, we've come no further. Samhain isn't evil spirits. It isn't goblins, ghosts or witches. It's the unconscious mind. We're all afraid of the dark inside ourselves.

61. What kind of plastic surgery did Dr. Loomis tell Dr. Wynn he got due to his encounters with Michael Myers from the past?
    a. Skin Grafts
    b. Facial Contouring
    c. Facial Rejuvenation
    d. Body Contouring

62. Who does Dr. Wynn plan on using to replace Michael Myers with the Curse of Thorn?
    a. Danny Strode
    b. Jamie Lloyd
    c. Tommy Doyle
    d. Stephen

63. In the producer's cut of the film, who was under the mask of Michael Myers when Michael escaped?
    a. Dr. Terrence Wynn
    b. Tommy Doyle
    c. Dr. Sam Loomis
    d. Mrs. Blankenship

64. In the producer's cut of the film, who does Dr. Wynn tell Michael his final sacrifice is?
    a. Stephen
    b. Danny Strode
    c. Kara Strode
    d. Tommy Doyle

65. Whose bed did Tim and Beth make love in?
    a. Tim's nephew's bed
    b. Tim's sister's bed
    c. Tim's parents' bed
    d. Tim's bed

66. What type of help did Barry Simms tell Tommy there is for people like him over the phone?
    a. Electromagnetic Therapy
    b. Electroconvulsive Therapy
    c. Electroshock Therapy
    d. Electron Therapy

67. Besides Tommy, who was the other caller to Barry Simms' radio show that had a name?
    a. Duanne
    b. David
    c. Darren
    d. Dustin

68. How old did Tommy say he was when he saw Michael Myers?
    a. Seven Years Old
    b. Eight Years Old
    c. Nine Years Old
    d. Ten Years Old

69. Who played the role of Tim Strode?
    a. Bradford English
    b. Keith Bogart
    c. Paul Rudd
    d. Devin Gardner

70. What led Tommy into finding Jamie's baby?
    a. A trail of milk
    b. A trail of blood
    c. A trail of crumbs
    d. A trail of piss

71. How did Jamie get in touch with Dr. Loomis about Michael being alive and coming after her?
    a. She called him
    b. She called into the Barry Simms radio show
    c. She called 911
    d. She called Smith's Grove

72. At the end of the producer's cut of the film, what happens to Dr. Loomis?
    a. He is killed   c. He gets the Curse of Thorn tattoo
    b. He kills Dr. Wynn   d. He helps Michael escape

73. In the producer's cut of the film, how does Jamie die?
    a. Stabbed with a knife   c. Shot by Dr. Wynn
    b. Impaled on farming equipment   d. Throat slit

74. What was Debra Strode doing before she was killed?
    a. Dusting   c. Cooking
    b. Sweeping   d. Laundry

75. Where did Jamie go to hide from Michael Myers and call for help?
    a. Subway   c. Bus Terminal
    b. Airport   d. Factory

76. Before Jamie died, what were her last words to Michael?
    a. You will never get my baby, Michael
    b. You can't have the baby, Michael
    c. You will never be able to find the baby, Michael
    d. You will not kill my baby, Michael

77. Who played the role of Debra Strode?
    a. Marianne Hagan   c. Susan Swift
    b. Janice Knickrehm   d. Kim Darby

78. What did one of the signs say at the Halloween party?
    a. He will be back   c. He will return
    b. He will kill again   d. He will find us

79. Before Jamie called out to Dr. Loomis, what did Dr. Loomis think happened to her?
    a. She died in the explosion at the police station
    b. She was committed into a psychiatric institute
    c. She committed suicide
    d. She was in a car accident

80. What does Tommy look through out his window and into the Myers house?
    a. Telescope   c. Binoculars
    b. Magnifying Glass   d. Night Vision Goggles

81. What county is Smith's Grove Sanitarium in?
    a. Warren County   c. Schuylkill County
    b. Luzerne County   d. Wessex County

82. In the producer's cut of the film, what children's Christian tune is the little girl singing "Mommy it's raining, it's raining red"?
    a. Joy to the World
    b. Jesus Loves Me This I Know
    c. He's Got the Whole World in His Hands
    d. Away In A Manger

83. What did Dr. Loomis tell Debra Strode that Michael has at their house that makes it sacred to him?
    a. Feelings   c. Fits of Rage
    b. Memories   d. Nightmares

84. What did Debra Strode notice was gone to be alarmed that Michael Myers is nearby?
    a. Butcher Knife   c. Axe
    b. Scythe   d. Scissors

85. Who played the role of Beth?
    a. Kim Darby   c. Mariah O'Brien
    b. Marianne Hagan   d. J.C. Brandy

86. How many years have passed from the end of *Halloween 5: The Revenge of Michael Myers* to the current events in *Halloween: The Curse of Michael Myers*?
    a. Six Years   c. Five Years
    b. Seven Years   d. Ten Years

87. Who was revealed to be the one behind Michael's rage and final sacrifice with the Curse of Thorn?
    a. Dr. Sam Loomis   c. Mrs. Blankenship
    b. Tommy Doyle   d. Dr. Terrence Wynn

88. Who did Dr. Terrence Wynn have tied up in a crucifix for a Satanic Samhain ritual?
    a. Tommy Doyle   c. Danny Strode
    b. Stephen   d. Kara Strode

89. What symbol did the Man in Black carve into Jamie's baby in the beginning of the film?
    a. Thorn   c. Jack-o'-Lantern
    b. Ghost   d. Devil Horns

90. What was Jamie trying to tell the Motorist to do before Michael killed him?
    a. To get into the truck with her   c. To beware of Michael
    b. To run   d. To call for help

91. What did John Strode find odd about the washing machine when he was in the basement?
    a. It is running when the power is out   c. It leaked water all over the floor
    b. The clothes weren't getting cleaned   d. It wouldn't turn on

92. What incident featuring Tommy Doyle from the original *Halloween* film happened to Danny Strode in *Halloween: The Curse of Michael Myers*?
    a. Danny Strode kept telling Kara that he saw the Boogeyman
    b. Danny Strode tripped and smashed his jack-o'-lantern
    c. Danny Strode was followed by Michael Myers when leaving school
    d. Danny Strode ran out of the house calling for help when Michael was in the house with Kara

93. What did Jamie Lloyd have wrapped in the blanket instead of her baby to trick Michael?
    a. A Shirt   c. A Diaper
    b. A Pillow   d. A Towel

94. Why did Mary help Jamie to escape?
    a. So Michael wouldn't kill Jamie
    b. To help her escape the rituals
    c. So she can save her baby
    d. To keep her secret about her baby's daddy

95. What did Tim Strode do to prove his father's point on kids having no respect?
    a. He farted   c. He burped
    b. He snorted   d. He sneezed

96. Who gave Tim his towel after he finished his shower?
    a. Danny Strode   c. Michael Myers
    b. Beth   d. Dr. Terrence Wynn

97. Who played the role of John Strode?
    a. Leo Geter   c. Keith Bogart
    b. Mitchell Ryan   d. Bradford English

98. What did the end of the theater release of the film symbolize?
    a. Dr. Loomis was finally killed by Michael Myers due to the actor dying after filming concluded
    b. Dr. Loomis became the new evil of Haddonfield
    c. Dr. Loomis killed Dr. Terrence Wynn to put a stop to Michael once and for all
    d. Dr. Loomis finally was able to kill Michael Myers to end his reign of terror for good

99. Who did Kara see get killed in her bed?
    a. Beth   c. Tim Strode
    b. Debra Strode   d. John Strode

100. How does Michael Myers kill Tim Strode?
    a. Slits his throat with a hunting knife
    b. Slits his throat with a butcher knife
    c. Slits his throat with a glass shard
    d. Slits his throat with a pair of scissors

Halloween H20: 20 Years Later

1. Which actor/actress made their ultimate return to the *Halloween* franchise in *Halloween H20: 20 Years Later*?
    a. Brian Andrews   c. Jamie Lee Curtis
    b. Kyle Richards   d. Charles Cyphers

2. What was the budget of *Halloween H20: 20 Years Later*?
    a. $18,000,000   c. $17,000,000
    b. $15,000,000   d. $16,000,000

3. When was *Halloween H20: 20 Years Later* released into theaters?
    a. August 1, 1998   c. August 5, 1998
    b. August 3, 1998   d. August 12, 1998

4. What did *Halloween H20: 20 Years Later* make at the box office?
    a. $50,000,000   c. $55,000,000
    b. $60,000,000   d. $65,000,000

5. Who directed *Halloween H20: 20 Years Later*?
    a. John Carpenter   c. Steve Miner
    b. Tommy Lee Wallace   d. Dwight H. Little

6. What name is Laurie Strode going by?
    a. Keri Tate   c. Kimmy Tate
    b. Kathy Tate   d. Karen Tate

7. Who scares Laurie Strode and says "It's Halloween, everyone is entitled to one good scare" just like Sheriff Brackett did in the original *Halloween* film?
    a. Will Brennan   c. John Tate
    b. Norma Watson   d. Molly Cartwell

8. What is the name of the school that Laurie Strode works for?
    a. Hightop Academy   c. Honorwood Academy
    b. Hampton Academy   d. Hillcrest Academy

9. In the beginning of the film, she is now divorced and Michael finally kills her. She is the last of the original night in 1978 he needed to kill that was associated with Dr. Loomis. Who is she?
    a. Lindsay Wallace   c. Marion Chambers
    b. Laurie Strode   d. Darlene Carruthers

10. Where did everyone go for the class field trip?
    a. Zion National Park   c. Yosemite National Park
    b. Yellowstone National Park   d. Redwood National Park

11. At the end of the film, what did Ronny tell his wife he wanted to write?
    a. Romantic Comedy   c. Docudrama
    b. Horror Comedy   d. Romantic Thriller

12. What was written on the chalkboard as Laurie taught the class?
    a. The Purgatory of C.S. Lewis, Where Does It Begin?
    b. The Purgatory of W.B. Yeats, Where Does It Begin?
    c. The Sinking of the Titanic, Where Does It Begin?
    d. The Diary of Anne Frank, Where Does It Begin?

13. What was the name of the town that Marion lived in?
    a. Langdon, Illinois   c. Russellville, Illinois
    b. Ridgemont, Illinois   d. Haddonfield, Illinois

14. What was Molly's advice to Laurie about fate, based on her answer in class?
    a. If it was fate, it must be conquered
    b. If it was fate, it must be faced
    c. If it was fate, it must be meant to happen
    d. If it was fate, it must be destined

15. What unusual object did Laurie stab Michael with?
    a. American Flag   c. Boy Scouts Flag
    b. California State Flag   d. Hillcrest Academy Flag

16. What was the number of the highway Michael was driving on and where was it precisely located?
    a. Highway 140, Northern California
    b. Highway 135, Northern California
    c. Highway 139, Northern California
    d. Highway 141, Northern California

17. What was Marion's street address?
    a. 4238 Cypress Pond Road   c. 4946 Cypress Pond Road
    b. 4752 Cypress Pond Road   d. 4118 Cypress Pond Road

18. What was the name of the town that the school is located in?
    a. Big Bear, California   c. Summer Glen, California
    b. Claremont, California   d. Inglewood, California

19. What rapper played the role of Ronny Jones?
    a. Will Smith   c. LL Cool J
    b. Usher   d. Snoop Dogg

20. Who voiced the role of Dr. Sam Loomis in the beginning of the film?
    a. Donald Pleasence   c. Malcolm McDowell
    b. Tom Kane   d. Steve Miner

21. What was Will Brennan's job title at Hillcrest Academy?
    a. Physics Teacher   c. Dean of Students
    b. Guidance Counselor   d. Assistant Principal

22. What was the body count in *Halloween H20: 20 Years Later*?
    a. Seven   c. Eight
    b. Six   d. Nine

23. In *Halloween (1978)*, Laurie Strode tells Tommy and Lindsay to go down the street to the McKenzie's house. In *Halloween H20: 20 Years Later*, Laurie Strode tells John and Molly to go down the street to whose house, in reference to the 1996 film *Scream*?
    a. Becker's   c. Campbell's
    b. Weathers'   d. Riley's

24. Who played Michael Myers in *Halloween H20: 20 Years Later*?
    a. Christopher Durand   c. Brad Loree
    b. George P. Wilbur   d. Don Shanks

25. Who role was P.J. Soles, who played Lynda in *Halloween (1978)*, supposed to play?
    a. Molly Cartwell   c. Sarah Wainthrope
    b. Keri Tate   d. Norma Watson

26. What is the first name of Ronny's wife?
    a. Shirley   c. Sharon
    b. Shannon   d. Sherry

27. What is Laurie Strode, under the name of Keri Tate's, job title at Hillcrest Academy?
    a. Psychology Teacher   c. Principal
    b. Headmistress   d. Superintendent

28. Which film directed by Steve Miner, did Jamie Lee Curtis first work with him?
    a. Friday the 13th Part 2   c. Forever Young
    b. Night of the Creeps   d. Warlock

29. What was the original working title for *Halloween H20: 20 Years Later*?
    a. Halloween 7: The Return of Laurie Strode
    b. Halloween 7: Laurie vs. Michael
    c. Halloween 7: The Life of Laurie Strode
    d. Halloween 7: The Revenge of Laurie Strode

30. How did Laurie "kill" Michael Myers at the end of the film?
    a. She beheaded Michael with an axe
    b. She had him blown up in an exploding ambulance
    c. She stabbed him repeatedly in the face
    d. She gave him a lethal injection

31. What happened to Jamie Lee Curtis one month after the film's release?
    a. She was stalked by a man in a Michael Myers costume
    b. She got a star on the Hollywood Walk of Fame
    c. She got labeled as a true horror "Scream Queen"
    d. She was inducted into the Horror Hall of Fame

32. Who played the role of Will Brennan?
    a. Adam Arkin   c. LL Cool J
    b. Josh Hartnett   d. Joseph Gordon-Levitt

33. John Tate turned the same age that Laurie's sister was when she was killed by Michael. She now knows that Michael will be coming after him due to that age. How old did John turn?
    a. Fifteen   c. Sixteen
    b. Seventeen   d. Eighteen

34. Who did Laurie Strode shoot thinking it was her brother?
    a. Ronny Jones   c. Will Brennan
    b. Norma Watson   d. Charlie Deveraux

35. How many times did Jimmy say he was suspended for getting a little crazy with a hockey stick?
    a. Three   c. Five
    b. Four   d. Six

36. What children's song was the little girl humming in the bathroom?
    a. Itsy Bitsy Spider
    b. Humpty Dumpty
    c. Mary Had a Little Lamb
    d. Patty Cake

37. What famous slasher film is Janet Leigh, who plays Norma, most noticeable for starring in?
    a. Friday the 13th (1980)
    b. Psycho
    c. A Nightmare on Elm Street (1984)
    d. The Texas Chainsaw Massacre

38. Why isn't Charlie going to Yosemite?
    a. He flunked his Algebra midterm exam
    b. He was turned down for his scholarship
    c. He didn't hand in his History report
    d. He never got his permission slip signed

39. What time do the buses leave for Yosemite?
    a. 4:30 Sharp   c. 4:15 Sharp
    b. 4:45 Sharp   d. 4:00 Sharp

40. Why did Will Brennan say he cannot join the girls for a night of fun?
    a. It isn't professional   c. He is having his nipples pierced
    b. He has a date   d. He has to make his rounds

41. What did Molly hit Michael with when she was just about to kill John?
    a. Log   c. Rock
    b. Cinder Block   d. Brick

42. What did Ronny's wife say is not working out for him?
    a. His job as a security guard   c. His career as a writer
    b. His marriage with her   d. His moves during sex

43. When Will asked Laurie why she didn't want to go camping, what did she say her reason was?
    a. It sounds like a blast   c. It sounds like a great time
    b. It sounds like fun   d. It sounds like a hoot

44. What kind of addict is John's father?
    a. Heroin   c. Cocaine
    b. Pill Popping   d. Methadone

45. How many months late is the birthday card John got from his father?
    a. One Month   c. Three Months
    b. Five Months   d. Two Months

46. Who played the role of Jimmy Howell?
    a. Adam Hann-Byrd   c. Joseph Gordon-Levitt
    b. Josh Hartnett   d. Adam Arkin

47. What is Norma Watson's job title at Hillcrest Academy?
    a. Secretary   c. Vice Principal
    b. Calculus Teacher   d. Lunch Monitor

48. Why did the little girl scream in the bathroom?
    a. She saw Michael Myers   c. She saw a spider
    b. She fell in the toilet   d. She heard someone walk in

49. How did Sarah get out of going to Yosemite?
    a. She has a fever of 102 and has to stay in bed all weekend long
    b. She has a death in the family and has to go back to her hometown
    c. She got a job and cannot get the weekend off of work
    d. She promised to take her little brother Trick-or-Treating

50. What kind of white wine was Laurie drinking while on lunch with Will?
    a. Semillon   c. Chardonnay
    b. Sauvignon Blanc   d. Pinot Grigio

51. What were the five things that Laurie told Will she tried to recover from her past?
    a. 12-Steps, Self Help, Group Therapy, Shrinks, and Yoga
    b. 12-Steps, Self Help, Group Therapy, Shrinks, and Meditation
    c. 12-Steps, Self Help, Group Therapy, Shrinks, and Kickboxing
    d. 12-Steps, Self Help, Group Therapy, Shrinks, and Fear Counseling

52. What book did the class read as a homework assignment, assigned by Laurie?
    a. Bram Stoker's Dracula   c. Of Mice and Men
    b. Mary Shelley's Frankenstein   d. Beowulf

53. When Laurie got into her car, what song played on the radio?
    a. Monster Mash   c. The Addams Family
    b. Mr. Sandman   d. I Will Survive

54. Which actress from *Scream 2* is seen on the television in the Molly and Sarah's bedroom?
    a. Neve Campbell   c. Sarah Michelle Gellar
    b. Courtney Cox-Arquette   d. Laurie Metcalf

55. LL Cool J wasn't just playing a security guard who is also a writer. What did LL Cool J do a month after the film was released?
    a. He had a fiction novel published
    b. He had a romantic thriller novel published
    c. He had a biographical novel published
    d. He had an autobiography published

56. What word was Michael originally supposed to speak at the end of the film before it was cut from the final script?
    a. Sister   c. Sis
    b. Laurie   d. Help

57. In the original script, who was Ronny going to be?
    a. A female named Hattie   c. A female named Hillary
    b. A female named Haley   d. A female named Heidi

58. What did Will tell Laurie he is great at that may be helpful for her recovery?
    a. Listening   c. Giving Advice
    b. Giving Motivational Speeches   d. Giving Encouragement

59. Who played the role of Charlie Deveraux?
    a. Joseph Gordon-Levitt   c. Josh Hartnett
    b. Adam Hann-Byrd   d. LL Cool J

60. Which main character was supposed to be killed off but survived in the final script?
    a. John Tate   c. Laurie Strode
    b. Norma Watson   d. Molly Cartwell

61. What movie was playing on the television when Marion found Jimmy's corpse?
    a. Plan 9 from Outer Space
    b. The Thing
    c. ET: The Extra-Terrestrial
    d. Alien

62. What is Marion's surname now that she is divorced?
    a. Williamson
    b. Whittington
    c. Wallace
    d. Washington

63. In the original script, Marion was not going to be in the film. In her place, a new character would be introduced as Dr. Loomis' daughter. What was his daughter's name going to be when written in the original script?
    a. Rochelle Loomis
    b. Rachel Loomis
    c. Rosie Loomis
    d. Renata Loomis

64. P.J. Soles was originally supposed to portray Norma Watson because she played a character named Norma Watson in which classic horror film?
    a. April Fool's Day
    b. Final Exam
    c. Carrie
    d. Sleepaway Camp

65. Who played the role of Molly Cartwell?
    a. Nancy Stephens
    b. Janet Leigh
    c. Jodi Lyn O'Keefe
    d. Michelle Williams

66. In an original draft of the film written by Daniel Farrands, there was going to be a student who did a book report on a book titled what that would tie in all of the films of the franchise?
    a. The Curse of Haddonfield
    b. The Michael Myers Legend
    c. The Halloween Murders
    d. Evil Never Dies

67. In the beginning of the film, what is the date?
    a. October 25, 1998
    b. October 29, 1998
    c. October 30, 1998
    d. October 31, 1998

68. Janet Leigh, as Norma Watson, is her first role in a major film in how many years?
    a. Fifteen Years
    b. Ten Years
    c. Twenty Years
    d. Eighteen Years

69. Which popular film did Josh Hartnett star in a few years after his success in *Halloween H20: 20 Years Later*?
    a. Pearl Harbor
    b. Black Hawk Down
    c. Shrek
    d. Ocean's Eleven

70. What type of school is Hillcrest Academy?
    a. Private University
    b. Private Boarding School
    c. Catholic High School
    d. Community College

71. Where does Sarah find Charlie's corpse?
    a. Stuffed in the refrigerator
    b. In the kitchen dumbwaiter
    c. On the kitchen floor
    d. Under the kitchen table

72. What did Michael use to kill Jimmy?
    a. Hockey Stick   c. Ice Skate
    b. Butcher Knife   d. Fireplace Poker

73. What did Michael steal from Marion's house?
    a. His diagnosis from Dr. Loomis
    b. His family history
    c. Information on Jamie Lloyd
    d. A file regarding Laurie Strode

74. What films of the *Halloween* franchise does this film ignore?
    a. Halloween 3 to 6   c. Halloween 1 and 2
    b. Halloween 4 and 5   d. Halloween 3

75. Who played the role of Sarah Wainthrope?
    a. Jodi Lyn O'Keefe   c. Michelle Williams
    b. Lisa Gay Hamilton   d. Jamie Lee Curtis

76. What was Ronny's job at the school?
    a. Security Guard   c. Custodian
    b. Groundskeeper   d. Hall Monitor

77. What does Laurie steal at the end of the film to make sure Michael is killed once and for all?
    a. Ambulance   c. Police Car
    b. Coroner's Van   d. School Bus

78. Where does Michael hang Sarah's corpse?
    a. School Parking Lot   c. Hallway
    b. Basement   d. Pantry

79. What did Michael embed into Charlie's throat to kill him?
    a. Bottle Opener   c. Pocket Knife
    b. Pizza Cutter   d. Corkscrew

80. Where were John, Molly, Charlie, and Sarah hosting their intimate Halloween party?
    a. Cafeteria   c. Classroom
    b. Gymnasium   d. Basement

81. Early in the film, what is revealed about Laurie Strode?
   a. Laurie faked her death and went into hiding
   b. Laurie changed her name to avoid being found by Michael Myers
   c. Laurie never had a daughter named Jamie
   d. Laurie still has night terrors about her encounter with Michael 20 years ago

82. What is the official tagline of the film?
   a. This summer, terror won't be taking a vacation
   b. 20 years later, he comes home one last time
   c. He is back and this time, he finds who he wants
   d. Michael is back and he is thirsty for blood

83. Who produced *Halloween H20: 20 Years Later*?
   a. Daryn Okada   c. Paul Freeman
   b. Patrick Lussier   d. Robert Zappia

84. Molly and Sarah were watching *Scream 2* in their room, however, what were they watching
in the original script before it was changed to *Scream 2* in postproduction?
   a. When A Stranger Calls   c. A Nightmare on Elm Street
   b. The Texas Chainsaw Massacre   d. So I Married an Axe Murderer

85. Which actor/actress made his film debut in *Halloween H20: 20 Years Later*?
   a. Adam Hann-Byrd   c. Josh Hartnett
   b. Michelle Williams   d. Joseph Gordon-Levitt

86. Which line from the film was ad-libbed by LL Cool J due to Josh Hartnett's messy haircut?
   a. Comb your hair   c. Wash your hair
   b. Cut your hair   d. Do something to your hair

87. Why is the film titled *Halloween H20*?
   a. Because the film is a family feud and the old saying says "blood is thicker than water"
   with H20 being the chemical symbol for water
   b. Because the H stands for Halloween and the 20 stands for 20 years later
   c. Because H20 is the chemical symbol of water which has a pH balance of 7.0 and this is the
   seventh film in the franchise
   d. Because this film is classified as a direct sequel to the original film in 1978 and the H20
   stands for Halloween 2.0

88. Who played the role of John Tate?
   a. Josh Hartnett   c. Adam Hann-Byrd
   b. Joseph Gordon-Levitt   d. Branden Williams

89. Which actor has a small role as a detective but was removed in the final draft of the script?
   a. Charles S. Dutton   c. Michael Clark Duncan
   b. Jeff Goldblum   d. Ed Harris

90. When Laurie catches John and Charlie what they're doing off campus what does John reply with?
    a. Getting a little off campus lunch
    b. Getting an anniversary gift for Molly
    c. Getting some Halloween decorations for the party
    d. Getting some fresh air

91. Why did John and Charlie sneak off campus?
    a. They shoplifted some intimate items for their dates with Molly and Sarah
    b. They shoplifted some booze
    c. They shoplifted some Halloween decorations
    d. They shoplifted some jewelry for their girlfriends

92. Why was Laurie so pissed off and upset that John snuck off campus?
    a. Because California is a big state
    b. Because she can get in trouble with being the school's headmistress
    c. Because it is Halloween and she is fearful of Michael's return
    d. Because he can get kicked out of Hillcrest Academy for breaking the code of conduct

93. What did John say to Charlie that his mom is?
    a. A strict teacher   c. A vulnerable mother
    b. A scared little girl   d. A functioning alcoholic

94. How old was Laurie Strode when Michael came after her 20 years ago?
    a. Seventeen   c. Sixteen
    b. Eighteen   d. Nineteen

95. What did Norma tell Laurie is clogged again?
    a. The pipes in the boy's restroom
    b. The drains in the girl's shower room
    c. The toilets in the boy's locker room
    d. The sinks in the girl's restroom

96. What did John tell Ronny he wanted to get off campus?
    a. A gift for Molly for their date   c. Candles and flowers for Molly
    b. Condoms for his romantic night with Molly   d. Chocolates for Molly

97. What did Ronny say would happen to him at the hands of Laurie if he let John off campus again?
    a. He'd have his neck rung by her   c. He'd be suspended
    b. He'd lose his security license   d. He'd be fired

98. Who does Laurie keep visioning as Michael Myers?
    a. Will Brennan   c. Norma Watson
    b. John Tate   d. Ronny Jones

99. When Will asks Laurie "what do we do?" when they are running from Michael, what does Laurie respond with?
    a. Try to live   c. Try to kill him
    b. Try to escape   d. Try to run

100. Why can't Molly go to Yosemite?
    a. Because her dad flaked on her financial aid
    b. Because she never got her permission slip signed
    c. Because she plagiarized her book report
    d. Because she didn't maintain a B average

Halloween: Resurrection

1. What was the budget of *Halloween: Resurrection*?
   a. $10,000,000
   b. $11,000,000
   c. $15,000,000
   d. $13,000,000

2. Who played Michael Myers in *Halloween: Resurrection*?
   a. Christopher Durand
   b. Tyler Mane
   c. Brad Loree
   d. Nick Castle

3. When was *Halloween: Resurrection* released into theaters?
   a. July 12, 2002
   b. July 12, 2000
   c. July 12, 2001
   d. July 12, 2003

4. Who directed *Halloween: Resurrection*?
   a. Rick Rosenthal
   b. John Carpenter
   c. Moustapha Akkad
   d. Steve Miner

5. What was the body count of *Halloween: Resurrection*?
   a. Five
   b. Eight
   c. Seven
   d. Ten

6. What was Deckard's real name?
   a. Mikey Barton
   b. Mario Barton
   c. Myles Barton
   d. Max Barton

7. How did Michael escape his beheading at Hillcrest as explained by the nurses?
   a. He is immortal and thus never dies, even with a beheading
   b. He crushed a guard's larynx and switched uniforms with him
   c. He put a mechanical robot in his mask and attire and left unscathed
   d. He was resurrected by the Curse of Thorn

8. What is the name of the show that will star all six students?
   a. Dangertainment
   b. Famoustainment
   c. Hallotainment
   d. Riskytainment

9. Rudy pointed out that all the stuff they find is "too easy". Where did it come from?
   a. Most of the props were placed in the house by a delivering company
   b. Most of the props were placed in the house by intern students
   c. Most of the props were placed in the house by warehouse workers
   d. Most of the props were placed in the house by Freddie and his staff

10. What was Jen's motive for participating on the show?
    a. She hopes to find a boyfriend
    b. She hopes to get noticed by Hollywood through her performance
    c. She hopes to give a kick ass performance and entertain the audience
    d. She hopes to find Michael Myers

11. What became of Laurie after the incident at Hillcrest?
    a. She discovered she beheaded the wrong man and committed suicide
    b. She discovered she beheaded the wrong man and became a pill popper
    c. She discovered she beheaded the wrong man and was committed to a psychiatric sanitarium
    d. She discovered she beheaded the wrong man and began having night terrors

12. Who was Freddie's favorite Kung Fu actor?
    a. Bruce Lee   c. Wai Chung Lee
    b. Jackie Chan   d. Vincent Zhao

13. What was the name of the song and artist that Nora jammed to while Charley was killed?
    a. Hot in Herre by Nelly   c. All For You by Janet Jackson
    b. If Tomorrow Never Comes by Ronan Keating   d. Still Waiting by Sum 41

14. What was Donna's theory surrounding Michael Myers?
    a. That Michael Myers had an impulse control disorder, prompting his never-ending thirst to kill
    b. That Michael Myers had an obsessive compulsive disorder, prompting his never-ending thirst to kill
    c. That Michael Myers had an attention deficit disorder, prompting his never-ending thirst to kill
    d. That Michael Myers had a post-traumatic stress disorder, prompting his never-ending thirst to kill

15. What was the name of the mental patient that cites the biography of serial killers?
    a. Willie   c. Harold
    b. Aron   d. Charley

16. What was the original working title of *Halloween: Resurrection*?
    a. Halloween: The Homecoming
    b. Halloween: The Reunion
    c. Halloween: The Return
    d. Halloween: The Revival

17. Which actor that was in this film for a small role was also in a much bigger role in *Freddy vs. Jason*?
    a. Jason Ritter   c. Brendan Fletcher
    b. Chris Gauthier   d. Kyle Labine

18. Who does Laurie Strode have a picture of hanging on the wall above her bed?
    a. Will Brennan   c. Jamie Lloyd
    b. John Tate   d. Jimmy

19. Laurie Strode is only in the film for 15 minutes. How many lines of dialogue does she speak within those 15 minutes?
    a. Ten   c. Twelve
    b. Eleven   d. Thirteen

20. Dr. Mixter, who is also the name of the doctor in *Halloween 2 (1981)*, is a different character that is a professor of which field at Haddonfield University?
    a. Sociology   c. Anatomy and Physiology
    b. Psychology   d. Human Biology

21. Who did Dr. Mixter cite when he said "We must face down our fears and face up to the figure"?
    a. Sigmund Freud   c. Carl Jung
    b. Carl Rogers   d. Albert Ellis

22. What was Rudy's major at Haddonfield University?
    a. Pastry Arts   c. Culinary Arts
    b. Graphic Art   d. Theatre

23. What was the last thing Laurie said to Michael Myers before plummeting to her death?
    a. You won't win, Michael
    b. You will die, Michael
    c. I'll see you in hell
    d. I still love you

24. What was the name of the cameraman?
    a. Charley Albans   c. Bill Woodlake
    b. Jim Morgan   d. Franklin Munroe

25. What rapper played the role of Freddie Harris?
    a. LL Cool J   c. Busta Rhymes
    b. Will Smith   d. Dr. Dre

26. Who was the final girl of *Halloween: Resurrection*?
    a. Donna Chang   c. Sara Moyer
    b. Laurie Strode   d. Jenna Danzig

27. What two directors turned down the opportunity to direct *Halloween: Resurrection*?
    a. John Carpenter and Dwight H. Little
    b. Whitney Ransick and Dwight H. Little
    c. Tommy Lee Wallace and Dwight H. Little
    d. Rob Zombie and Dwight H. Little

28. Freddie's last name was given to him in homage of which actress that previously starred in a *Halloween* film?
    a. Ellie Cornell   c. Jamie Lee Curtis
    b. Tamara Glynn   d. Danielle Harris

29. Which actress in *Halloween: Resurrection* was originally supposed to play the role of Donna Chang but was given a different character instead?
    a. Katee Sackhoff   c. Tyra Banks
    b. Bianca Kajlich   d. Lorena Gale

30. Which actress was scheduled to play Sara Moyer in *Halloween: Resurrection* but dropped out of the role shortly before production began?
    a. Jennifer Love Hewitt   c. Sarah Michelle Gellar
    b. Drew Barrymore   d. Jacinda Barrett

31. Nora's death was a reference to which nurse's death in *Halloween 2*?
    a. Mrs. Alves   c. Nurse Janet Marshall
    b. Nurse Jill Franco   d. Nurse Karen Bailey

32. The ending was left opened for another sequel which would've had what type of storyline according to Moustapha Akkad?
    a. John Tate would return to avenge his mother's death
    b. John Tate would return to find his mother that he believes faked her death again
    c. John Tate would return as the next intended target for Michael
    d. John Tate would return on a mission to kill Michael once and for all

33. Who played the role of Jim Morgan?
    a. Luke Kirby   c. Thomas Ian Nicholas
    b. Ryan Merriman   d. Brad Loree

34. Michael switching outfits with the paramedic which explained how he survived the end of *Halloween H20: 20 Years Later* is similar to the ending of which film in the franchise?
    a. Halloween 4: The Return of Michael Myers
    b. Halloween 3: Season of the Witch
    c. The Producer's Cut of Halloween 6: The Curse of Michael Myers
    d. Halloween 5: The Revenge of Michael Myers

35. What happened in this film that happened in a previous film of the *Halloween* franchise to Michael Myers, both directed by the same director?
    a. Michael's eyes opened
    b. Michael is set on fire
    c. Michael is shown unmasked
    d. Michael is shown as a boy

36. Who is Freddie dressed as to scare his students?
    a. Jason Voorhees   c. Michael Myers
    b. Freddy Krueger   d. Pinhead

37. Who did Rudy say was a vegetarian when talking about having a poor diet?
    a. Joseph Stalin   c. Adolf Hitler
    b. Osama Bin Laden   d. Benedict Arnold

38. Who told the story of what happened at the end of *Halloween H20: 20 Years Later*?
    a. Nurse Wells   c. Nurse Phillips
    b. Professor Mixter   d. Freddie Harris

39. What type of food did Rudy ask Michael if he liked when fighting him right before his death?
    a. Chicken Fried Rice   c. Pizza
    b. Tacos   d. Sushi

40. What did Freddie tell Sara is good to have when convincing her to not drop out of the contest at the Myers house?
    a. Panic   c. Danger
    b. Fear   d. Nervousness

41. What is the name of the guy that attends Haddonfield University that told the story of Michael as a kid when talking about the Myers house?
    a. Aron   c. Harold
    b. Willie   d. Franklin

42. What did Freddie tell Sara the American dream is?
    a. Being Rich   c. Being Famous
    b. Being Successful   d. Being Loved

43. When Jenna screamed, what did Jim say she must be going for?
    a. The first Internet Emmy   c. The first Webby
    b. The first Scream Award   d. The title of Scream Queen

44. What did Donna say she is interested in about Michael Myers?
    a. How Michael Myers embodies the politics of violence embedded in Greek mythology
    b. How Michael Myers embodies the politics of violence embedded in pop mythology
    c. How Michael Myers embodies the politics of violence embedded in folk mythology
    d. How Michael Myers embodies the politics of violence embedded in Norse mythology

45. Who played the role of Myles Barton?
    a. Ryan Merriman   c. Billy Kay
    b. Sean Patrick Thomas   d. Gus Lynch

46. How many endings were shot regarding the fate of Freddie Harris?
    a. One   c. Three
    b. Two   d. Four

47. Who's Halloween party did Myles go to?
    a. Mickey Stern   c. Michael Shoffler
    b. Mario Sampson   d. Max Steele

48. What grade is Myles in?
    a. Sophomore in High School   c. Senior in High School
    b. Freshman in High School   d. Junior in College

49. What did Myles' friend's sister invite them to the Halloween party?
    a. So her mother doesn't find out she has a boyfriend
    b. So her mother doesn't find out she is pregnant
    c. So her mother doesn't find out about the party
    d. So her mother doesn't find out about her tattoo

50. Who played the role of Nora Winston?
    a. Lorena Gale   c. Katee Sackhoff
    b. Daisy McCrackin   d. Tyra Banks

51. Which actress in *Halloween: Resurrection* was originally supposed to play the role of Jenna
Danzig but was given a different character instead?
    a. Daisy McCrackin   c. Lorena Gale
    b. Tyra Banks   d. Bianca Kajlich

52. When Nora asks Jenna what she hopes to find in the Myers house, what does she say?
    a. Michael Myers himself
    b. Her way into network broadcasting
    c. The truth behind the evil within Michael Myers
    d. A passing grade

53. What did Bill Woodlake say about Michael Myers during his audition with Dangertainment?
    a. He is the great white shark of our unconscious, he is the dark-eyed guy of our spirits, he's
    every murderous impulse we had, he's the little voice that whispers to us to strangle the old
    lady trying to cross the street in busy traffic
    b. He is the great white shark of our unconscious, he is the dark-eyed guy of our spirits, he's
    every murderous impulse we had, he's the little voice that whispers to us to strangle the old
    lady that is being robbed for her purse by a street thug
    c. He is the great white shark of our unconscious, he is the dark-eyed guy of our spirits, he's
    every murderous impulse we had, he's the little voice that whispers to us to strangle the old
    lady that is taking too long at the checkout counter
    d. He is the great white shark of our unconscious, he is the dark-eyed guy of our spirits, he's
    every murderous impulse we had, he's the little voice that whispers to us to strangle the old
    lady that is a loving grandmother in the park with her grandchild

54. What was Sara's answer to Nora's question on why ordinary people turn to murder?
    a. It has to do with upbringing and then the photographer knocked over a light and she screamed, not being able to finish answering the question
    b. It has to do with lack of discipline and then the photographer knocked over a light and she screamed, not being able to finish answering the question
    c. It has to do with family values and then the photographer knocked over a light and she screamed, not being able to finish answering the question
    d. It has to do with the environment surrounding him and then the photographer knocked over a light and she screamed, not being able to finish answering the question

55. Who played the role of Rudy Grimes?
    a. Dan Joffre   c. Sean Patrick Thomas
    b. Brent Chapman   d. Ryan Merriman

56. Which of the two on Dangertainment got high while in the Myers house?
    a. Rudy Grimes and Jenna Danzig
    b. Rudy Grimes and Sara Moyer
    c. Rudy Grimes and Donna Chang
    d. Rudy Grimes and Nora Winston

57. What did Freddie say Michael looked like when he was burnt on the stretcher?
    a. Chicken Leg   c. Chicken Breast
    b. Chicken Wing   d. Chicken Fried

58. Who's corpse did Sara find on the roof of the Myers house?
    a. Nora Winston   c. Bill Woodlake
    b. Charley Albans   d. Laurie Strode

59. How many butcher knives did Michael stab Rudy with?
    a. One   c. Three
    b. Two   d. Four

60. What was the date in the film that Michael finally killed Laurie?
    a. October 31, 2002   c. October 31, 1999
    b. October 31, 2001   d. October 31, 2000

61. How did Sara, Jenna, Donna, Rudy, Jim, and Bill get to be on Dangertainment?
    a. They won a contest
    b. They were selected from a list of applicants
    c. They were recommended by the university committee
    d. They are all theater majors at the university

62. Laurie pretends to be what to prepare herself for the inevitable confrontation with Michael?
    a. Drunk   c. Insane
    b. Heavily Medicated   d. Comatose

63. When Jim and Donna are about to make love, the wall breaks with what falling on them?
    a. Fake Blood   c. Fake Corpses
    b. Fake Mice   d. Fake Spiders

64. What does Freddie say the audience will see when watching the Internet reality show on Dangertainment?
    a. The person holding the camera
    b. A falsified set up of the Myers house
    c. Only what the person holding the camera sees
    d. The hologram of Michael Myers

65. In 2003, Tyra Banks, who played Nora Winston, created which successful show on The CW Network/UPN?
    a. Project Runway   c. Shark Tank
    b. America's Next Top Model   d. The Real World

66. What is the name of Myles' friend?
    a. Sean   c. Scott
    b. Saxon   d. Shane

67. Who played the role of Jenna Danzig?
    a. Katee Sackhoff   c. Daisy McCrackin
    b. Marisa Rudiak   d. Kelly Nielson

68. After Michael killed Laurie, who did he give the butcher knife too?
    a. Nurse Phillips   c. Harold
    b. Nurse Wells   d. Bob Green

69. The girl that was flirting with Scott at the Halloween party was dressed as what?
    a. Devil   c. Cat
    b. French Maid   d. Cheerleader

70. Which of the following horror films did Sean Patrick Thomas, who played Rudy Grimes, star in?
    a. Dracula 2000   c. Final Destination
    b. Ginger Snaps   d. Scream 3

71. Who were the two nurses on duty the night Laurie Strode was killed?
    a. Nurse Wells and Nurse McCarthy
    b. Nurse Wells and Nurse Hunter
    c. Nurse Wells and Nurse Williamson
    d. Nurse Wells and Nurse Phillips

72. What was Nora Winston making when Charley was killed?
    a. Cappuccino   c. Frappuccino
    b. Mocha Latte   d. Espresso

73. Who played the role of Aron, the creepy student at Haddonfield University?
    a. Gus Lynch   c. Haig Sutherland
    b. David Lewis   d. Billy Kay

74. What car was parked outside the Myers house that Nora had towed?
    a. Viper   c. Cadillac
    b. Firebird   d. Porsche

75. In 2006, Ryan Merriman, who played Myles Barton, starred in which horror film sequel?
    a. The Texas Chainsaw Massacre: The Beginning
    b. The Grudge 2
    c. Final Destination 3
    d. I'll Always Know What You Did Last Summer

76. Jamie Lee Curtis, who played Laurie Strode, stars in which of the following horror television shows as Cathy Munsch?
    a. Scream   c. Scream Queens
    b. American Horror Story   d. The Walking Dead

77. Who played the role of Donna Chang?
    a. Charisse Baker   c. Natassia Malthe
    b. Daisy McCrackin   d. Katee Sackhoff

78. Which two popular horror films did Jamie Lee Curtis star in, excluding any of the *Halloween* films?
    a. Child's Play and A Nightmare on Elm Street
    b. The Fog and Prom Night
    c. The Texas Chainsaw Massacre and Scream
    d. Children of the Corn and Friday the 13th

79. When Freddie is being interviewed by the media, what did he say they were going to enter in about the next 10 minutes?
    a. A mystery wrapped inside of a riddle inside of an enigma
    b. A mystery wrapped inside of a riddle inside of a myth
    c. A mystery wrapped inside of a riddle inside of a legend
    d. A mystery wrapped inside of a riddle inside of a killer

80. What weapon is used in the Dangertainment logo?
    a. Butcher Knife   c. Machete
    b. Axe   d. Meat Cleaver

81. Who played the role of Bill Woodlake?
    a. Sean Patrick Thomas   c. Thomas Ian Nicholas
    b. Brad Sihvon   d. Haig Sutherland

82. What type of film was *Halloween: Resurrection*?
    a. Thriller   c. Suspense
    b. Mystery   d. Found Footage

83. Who came up with the idea for Busta Rhymes to star in the film?
    a. Jamie Lee Curtis' mother
    b. John Carpenter's brother
    c. Rick Rosenthal's wife
    d. Moustapha Akkad's son

84. How does the film end?
    a. Michael's cremated
    b. Michael's eyes opened in the morgue
    c. Michael kills the nurse
    d. Michael is gone from the morgue

85. What did Bill say that could launch Jenna's career and light up a thousand computer screens?
    a. If she had sex with him   c. If he flashed the camera
    b. If she stripped   d. If she faked her death

86. What did Michael use to impale Charley in the throat with?
    a. The leg of the tripod   c. A railroad spike
    b. A giant hook   d. A spear

87. In a deleted scene, what did Michael use to strangle Nora with before impaling her to the ceiling with a butcher knife?
    a. Cable Noose   c. Camera Wire
    b. His bare hands   d. Rope

88. When did Sara, Rudy, and Jim realize that Jenna wasn't faking her screams?
    a. When Michael decapitated her
    b. When they found a dead body
    c. When they saw Jenna soaked in blood
    d. When they saw two Michael Myers

89. Wat did Donna see in the basement that she thought was a prop of Freddie's?
    a. A dead skunk   c. A dead dog
    b. A dead cat   d. A dead rat

90. What did Jim see on the arm of the corpse that fell on him and Donna that made him realize the entire show was a set up from the beginning?
    a. The text "Made in China"
    b. The text "Made in Japan"
    c. The text "Made in Taiwan"
    d. The text "Made in Hong Kong"

91. Myles and Scott went to the Halloween party dressed as the characters of which film?
    a. Scarface   c. Pulp Fiction
    b. The Godfather   d. Goodfellas

92. When Myles was watching the Internet show by Dangertainment at the Halloween party, he was interrupted by two people making out. When the guy noticed Myles at the desk, what did he call him?
    a. Big Freak   c. Big Perv
    c. Big Daddy   d. Big Loser

93. What caused the Myers house to catch on fire when Sara was battling Michael?
    a. Sara set Michael on fire gasoline and a match
    b. Sara was attacking Michael with a chainsaw and struck live wires
    c. Sara had Michael knocked out and used gasoline and a match to light the place on fire
    d. Sara blew the place up with propane when she escaped the house

94. Who played the role of Sara Moyer?
    a. Daisy McCrackin   c. Bianca Kajlich
    b. Katee Sackhoff   d. Tyra Banks

95. What caused Laurie to be tricked by Michael and ultimately killed?
    a. She was fearful that it wasn't the real Michael like the last time
    b. She was feeling remorse for everything her brother has been through
    c. She was feeling doubt on killing her flesh and blood
    d. She thought Michael wanted to start over with her

96. What mask did Harold wear?
    a. Jack-o'-Lantern   c. Skeleton
    b. Clown   d. Michael Myers

97. What did Laurie hide in the doll?
    a. Pictures of her son   c. Her pills
    b. Memories of Michael's attacks on her   d. A secret weapon

98. What did the nurse say Laurie Strode suffers from?
    a. Post-Traumatic Stress Disorder   c. Extreme Dissociative Disorder
    d. Depression   b. Bipolar Disorder

99. What does the doctor think Laurie is?
    a. A homicidal maniac   c. A suicide threat
    b. A runaway patient   d. A dangerous person

100. What did *Halloween: Resurrection* make at the box office?
    a. $37.5 million   c. $37.7 million
    b. $37.3 million   d. $37.6 million

Halloween (2007)

1. Who played Dr. Sam Loomis in *Halloween (2007)*?
   a. Brad Dourif
   b. John Hurt
   c. Malcolm McDowell
   d. Donald Pleasence

2. What was the budget of *Halloween (2007)*?
   a. $15,000,000
   b. $10,000,000
   c. $20,000,000
   d. $25,000,000

3. When was *Halloween (2007)* released into theaters?
   a. August 12, 2007
   b. August 1, 2007
   c. August 31, 2007
   d. August 16, 2007

4. Who was the final girl of *Halloween (2007)*?
   a. Annie Brackett
   b. Lynda Van Der Klok
   c. Laurie Strode
   d. Judith Myers

5. What did *Halloween (2007)* make at the box office?
   a. $80.7 million
   b. $80.5 million
   c. $80.2 million
   d. $80.8 million

6. Who played Michael Myers in *Halloween (2007)*?
   a. Nick Castle
   b. Tyler Mane
   c. Kane Hodder
   d. Dick Warlock

7. Who directed *Halloween (2007)*?
   a. John Carpenter
   b. Steve Miner
   c. Malek Akkad
   d. Rob Zombie

8. What was the body count of *Halloween (2007)*?
   a. Seventeen
   b. Eighteen
   c. Nineteen
   d. Twenty

9. What was Michael's hobby?
   a. Painting
   b. Mask Making
   c. Sculpturing
   d. Photography

10. What were the circumstances surrounding Laurie's adoption?
    a. Sheriff Brackett found Laurie at the scene of Deborah's suicide, and she was later adopted by the Strodes
    b. Sheriff Brackett found Laurie at the scene of Deborah's suicide, and she was then put into foster care
    c. Sheriff Brackett found Laurie at the scene of Deborah's suicide, and immediately called Children and Youth
    d. Sheriff Brackett found Laurie at the scene of Deborah's suicide, and adopted her himself

11. What was the name of Dr. Loomis' book?
    a. The Eyes of Evil   c. The Devil's Eyes
    b. The Blackest Eyes   d. The Eyes of Pure Evil

12. During the film's opening moments, Michael wore a t-shirt of what band?
    a. AC/DC   c. KISS
    b. Metallica   d. Limp Bizkit

13. What song did both Judith and Lynda listen to right before their deaths?
    a. Bodies by Drowning Pool
    b. Don't Fear the Reaper by Blue Oyster Cult
    c. Feel So Numb by Rob Zombie
    d. St. Anger by Metallic

14. What obscenity was written on Ronnie's cast when he flipped off Deborah?
    a. Dumb Cunt   c. Suck It
    b. Stupid Bitch   d. Cheap Whore

15. What type of gun did Dr. Loomis buy from Mickey Dolenz?
    a. .32 Revolver   c. .357 Magnum
    b. .303 British   d. .45 Colt

16. What was the name of the cereal that Judith ate for breakfast?
    a. Fruity Pebbles   c. Cinnamon Toast Crunch
    b. Fruit Loops   d. Sugar Rice Pops

17. What type of costume did Laurie say she wore as a child?
    a. Witch   c. Bride of Frankenstein
    b. Zombie   d. Dead Little Red Riding Hood

18. Walking home from school, Lynda wore a t-shirt of what band?
    a. Avenge Sevenfold   c. Black Sabbath
    b. Judas Priest   d. Slayer

19. Who played the role of Annie Brackett?
    a. Kyle Richards   c. Danielle Harris
    b. Nancy Kyes   d. Jenny Gregg Stewart

20. Brad Dourif, who played Sheriff Brackett, starred as the villain of which horror franchise?
    a. Leprechaun   c. Child's Play
    b. Hellraiser   d. Candyman

21. Who played the role of Deborah Myers?
    a. Dee Wallace   c. Sheri Moon Zombie
    b. Hanna R. Hall   d. Patty Frost

22. At the start of the film, what was the quote shown on the screen by Dr. Sam Loomis?
    a. The evil souls are not those which choose to exist within the hell of the abyss, but those which choose to break free from the abyss and move silently among us
    b. The remorseful souls are not those which choose to exist within the hell of the abyss, but those which choose to break free from the abyss and move silently among us
    c. The darkest souls are not those which choose to exist within the hell of the abyss, but those which choose to break free from the abyss and move silently among us
    d. The deadly souls are not those which choose to exist within the hell of the abyss, but those which choose to break free from the abyss and move silently among us

23. Which actress auditioned for the role of Laurie Strode, but wasn't given the part?
    a. Emma Stone   c. Emma Roberts
    b. Billie Lourd   d. Abigail Breslin

24. Who played the role of Bob Simms?
    a. Travis Van Winkle   c. Glen Powell
    b. John Michael Graham   d. Nick Mennell

25. Skyler Gisondo auditioned for which role, but was instead cast as Tommy Doyle?
    a. Young Michael Myers   c. Wesley Rhoades
    b. Steve Haley   d. Paul

26. Where did Michael gets his infamous mask that he hid the night he killed his family?
    a. Under Judith's mattress   c. Under the house
    b. Under the floorboards   d. Under the welcome mat

27. Skyler Gisondo, who played Tommy Doyle, was also in the hit television show *Once Upon a Time* as which character?
    a. Felix   c. Devin
    b. Peter Pan   d. Michael Darling

28. What job does Deborah Myers do for a living?
    a. Dancer at a local strip club   c. Bartender
    b. Waitress   d. Hooker

29. Who played the role of Lynda Van Der Klok?
    a. Kristina Klebe   c. P.J. Soles
    b. Scout Taylor-Compton   d. Danielle Harris

30. What Stephen King horror film did Dee Wallace, who played Cynthia Strode, star in?
    a. IT   c. Cujo
    b. Children of the Corn   d. The Shining

31. What were the name of Laurie's adoptive parents?
    a. Mason and Cynthia Strode   c. Michael and Cynthia Strode
    b. Matthew and Cynthia Strode   d. Maxwell and Cynthia Strode

32. Who played the role of Sheriff Brackett?
    a. Charles Cyphers
    b. Beau Starr
    c. Hunter Von Leer
    d. Brad Dourif

33. What was the name of the truck driver that Michael killed for his clothes?
    a. Ismael Cruz
    b. Joe Grizzly
    c. Morgan Walker
    d. Noel Kluggs

34. What did Michael put over the head of Paul after he killed him?
    a. Pumpkin
    b. His Mask
    c. Plastic Bag
    d. TV Set

35. Danielle Harris, who played Annie Brackett, also starred in two other *Halloween* films as a child playing which character?
    a. Jamie Lloyd
    b. Samantha Thomas
    c. Lindsay Wallace
    d. Rachel Carruthers

36. What pet did Michael have as a kid?
    a. Rat
    b. Snake
    c. Dog
    d. Tarantula

37. What type of psychologist is Dr. Loomis?
    a. Human Psychologist
    b. Child Psychologist
    c. Behavior Psychologist
    d. Educational Psychologist

38. What does Michael use to make his masks?
    a. Clay
    b. Pottery
    c. Papier-mâché
    d. Putty

39. What did Michael say his favorite color is?
    a. White
    b. Gray
    c. Brown
    d. Black

40. What was Deborah's boyfriend's name?
    a. Larry Redgrave
    b. Stan Payne
    c. Zach Garrett
    d. Ronnie White

41. What was the name of the principal that tried to stop the fight between Michael and Wesley?
    a. Principal Carson
    b. Principal Chambers
    c. Principal Cox
    d. Principal Clinton

42. Who played the role of Judith Myers?
    a. Hanna R. Hall
    b. Sybil Danning
    c. Leslie Easterbrook
    d. Jenny Gregg Stewart

43. Before *Halloween 2007* became a remake of the original film, it was originally going to be a prequel titled what?
    a. Halloween: The Origin of Michael Myers
    b. Halloween: The Child Known As Michael Myers
    c. Halloween: The Missing Years
    d. Halloween: The Evil of Michael Myers

44. Who played the young Michael Myers in *Halloween (2007)*?
    a. Will Sandin   c. Daeg Faerch
    b. Skyler Gisondo   d. Chase Wright Vanek

45. Which classic film was playing on television in an early scene of *Halloween (2007)*?
    a. White Zombie   c. Citizen Kane
    b. Casablanca   d. The Wizard of Oz

46. The hoodie Laurie Strode wore in *Halloween (2007)* was from Sheri Moon Zombie's personal clothing line, which is what?
    a. The Walking Dead   c. Undead Attire
    b. Total Skull   d. Zombie Clothes

47. The sequel to this movie is *Halloween 2 (2009)*, but the original plan for a sequel was titled what?
    a. Halloween Returns   c. Halloween: Apocalypse
    b. Halloween: Retribution   d. Halloween: Emergence

48. Which actress that starred in *Friday the 13th (2009)* auditioned for the role of Laurie Strode, but lost the role to Scout Taylor-Compton?
    a. Amanda Righetti   c. Danielle Panabaker
    b. Julianna Guill   d. Willa Ford

49. Scout Taylor-Compton, who played Laurie Strode, auditioned for which role in *Friday the 13th (2009)*?
    a. Jenna   c. Whitney Miller
    b. Bree   d. Chelsea

50. Who played the role of Paul?
    a. Nick Mennell   c. Max Van Ville
    b. Daryl Sabara   d. Adam Weisman

51. In the opening scene of the film, which song by KISS was heard playing?
    a. Rock and Roll All Nite   c. God of Thunder
    b. Heaven's on Fire   d. Psycho Circus

52. Which character is the only one to not be killed by Michael Myers?
    a. Ronnie White   c. Wesley Rhoades
    b. Deborah Myers   d. Ismael Cruz

53. What does Dr. Loomis say about the eyes of Michael Myers when giving a speech about his book?

    a. c. I met him, fifteen years ago; I was told there was nothing left; no reason, no conscience, no understanding; and even the most rudimentary sense of life or death, of good or evil, right or wrong. I met this six-year-old child, with this blank, pale, emotionless face, and the blackest eyes... the devil's eyes. I spent eight years trying to reach him, and then another seven trying to keep him locked up because I realized that what was living behind that boy's eyes was purely and simply... evil.

    b. These eyes will deceive you, they will destroy you. They will take from you, your innocence, your pride, and eventually your soul. These eyes do not see what you and I see. Behind these eyes one finds only blackness, the absence of light, these are of a psychopath.

    c. These eyes will deceive you, they will destroy you, they will kill you. They will take from you, your innocence, your pride, and eventually your soul. These eyes do not see what you and I see. Behind these eyes one finds only blackness, the absence of light, these are of a psychopath. These are of a murderer. These are of someone who doesn't care if he lives or die. These eyes are of someone that is purely and simply…evil.

    d. These eyes will deceive you, they will destroy you. They will take from you, your innocence, your pride, your life, your self-respect, and eventually your soul. These eyes do not see what you and I see. Behind these eyes one finds only blackness, the absence of light, the forthcoming of darkness, these are of a psychopath. Someone so sinister, so evil that he doesn't care who or what he destroys and even kills. Someone he will kill without a second thought. The eyes that only make someone that is evil become so enraged in life.

54. Michael asked Dr. Loomis if he liked his mask and stated that black was his favorite color. Dr. Loomis told Michael that black isn't a color. When explaining why black isn't a color, Dr. Loomis stated what?

    a. It's the misinterpretation of color. In the spectrum of colors, you go from black, which is no color, all the way through to white, which is every color. So, technically... not that it really matters - but black isn't a color.

    b. It's the disappearance of color. In the spectrum of colors, you go from black, which is no color, all the way through to white, which is every color. So, technically... not that it really matters - but black isn't a color.

    c. It's the absence of color. In the spectrum of colors, you go from black, which is no color, all the way through to white, which is every color. So, technically... not that it really matters - but black isn't a color.

    d. It's the blindness of color. In the spectrum of colors, you go from black, which is no color, all the way through to white, which is every color. So, technically... not that it really matters - but black isn't a color.

55. Where did Dr. Loomis speak about his book on Michael Myers?

    a. Westminster Hall   c. Webster Hall
    b. Wyomissing Hall   d. Warner Hall

56. What time was on the sign of Dr. Loomis speaking about his book on Michael Myers?

    a. 11 AM   c. 12 PM Noon
    b. 10 AM   d. 1 PM

57. What was the name of the bully that picked on Michael Myers at school?
    a. Derek Allen   c. Wesley Rhoades
    b. Chester Chesterfield   d. Taylor Madison

58. What was the name of Michael's rat?
    a. Elvis   c. Erick
    b. Elias   d. Emeril

59. What name does Ronnie call Michael to make fun of him?
    a. Minnie   c. Mildred
    b. Michelle   d. Mimi

60. Which character that was only mentioned in *Halloween (1978)* was an actual on screen character in *Halloween (2007)*?
    a. Bob Simms   c. Steve Haley
    b. Deborah Myers   d. Paul

61. Sheriff Brackett told Dr. Loomis that it sounds like he is talking to who when he talks to Michael?
    a. The Devil   c. Satan
    b. The Antichrist   d. A Demon

62. Michael Myers hasn't spoken in how many years when he is shown as an adult?
    a. Twenty Years   c. Ten Years
    b. Fifteen Years   d. Twenty-Five Years

63. Max Van Ville, who played the role of Paul, originally auditioned for the role of which character?
    a. Bob Simms   c. Steve
    b. Wesley Rhoades   d. Joe Grizzly

64. Who played the role of Ronnie White?
    a. William Forsythe   c. Pat Skipper
    b. Ken Foree   d. Daniel Roebuck

65. What Halloween song did Lindsay keep singing?
    a. Trick or Treat. Smell my feet. Give me something good to eat. If you don't, I don't care. I'll pull down Laurie's underwear!
    b. Trick or Treat. Smell my feet. Give me something good to eat. If you don't, I don't care. I'll pull down Lynda's underwear!
    c. Trick or Treat. Smell my feet. Give me something good to eat. If you don't, I don't care. I'll pull down Tommy's underwear!
    d. Trick or Treat. Smell my feet. Give me something good to eat. If you don't, I don't care. I'll pull down Annie's underwear!

66. What were the three reasons Tommy told Laurie why Lindsay can't come over?
    a. 1: She's a girl.
       2: She's not a boy.
       3: She smells like Annie
    b. 1: She's a girl.
       2: She's not a boy.
       3: She smells like Lynda.
    c. 1: She's a girl.
       2: She's not a boy.
       3: She smells like you.
    d. 1: She's a girl.
       2: She's not a boy.
       3: She smells like shit.

67. When speaking to Michael while taking a dump, what did Joe Grizzly say he ate?
    a. Burrito   c. Taco Supreme
    b. Quesadilla   d. Enchiladas

68. What name did Joe Grizzly call Michael right before he went to attack Michael?
    a. Danielle   c. Daisy
    b. Demi   d. Dory

69. Why did Dr. Loomis tell Michael he couldn't go home?
    a. Because he has done terrible things
    b. Because he has done illegal things
    c. Because he has done dangerous things
    d. Because he has done bad things

70. When Michael was holding Laurie hostage, what did he show her?
    a. A picture of them, trying to tell her that he is her brother
    b. A picture of them, trying to tell her she is adopted
    c. A picture of them, trying to tell her that he killed her family
    d. A picture of them, trying to tell her that their family is dead and he's alone

71. Whose body did Laurie find?
    a. Cynthia Strode   c. Mason Strode
    b. Lynda Van Der Klok   d. Bob Simms

72. Who did Laurie find lying in a pool of her own blood, but she didn't die, unlike the original film?
    a. Lynda Van Der Klok   c. Annie Brackett
    b. Bob Simms   d. Paul

73. Who played the role of Steve Haley?
    a. Adam Weisman   c. Max Van Ville
    b. Nick Mennell   d. Daryl Sabara

74. Nick Mennell, who played Bob Simms, was also in what other classic slasher/horror movie remake?
    a. A Nightmare on Elm Street (2010)   c. Friday the 13th (2009)
    b. The Texas Chainsaw Massacre (2003)   d. Children of the Corn (2009)

75. Who played the role of Joe Grizzly?
    a. Paul Kampf   c. Richmond Arquette
    b. Ken Foree   d. Sid Haig

76. When did Michael first come face to face with Laurie Strode?
    a. When Laurie discovered the corpses of Lynda and Bob
    b. When Laurie discovered the corpse of Paul and an injured Annie
    c. When Laurie found out she is really Michael Myers' sister through Dr. Loomis' book
    d. When Laurie dropped off the key to the Myers' House for her dad

77. Who played the role of Wesley Rhoades?
    a. Daeg Faerch   c. Daryl Sabara
    b. Richard Lynch   d. Max Van Ville

78. Where did Deborah Myers work at?
    a. Rabbit in Red   c. The Rabbit Hole
    b. The Rabbit's Foot   d. Rabbit Ears

79. Which uncredited role did Ezra Buzzington play in *Halloween (2007)*?
    a. Graveyard Keeper   c. University Dean
    b. Drunk Patron   d. College Student

80. Deputy Charles was the same character in which previous *Halloween* film, just played by a different actor?
    a. Halloween 2 (1981)
    b. Halloween 4: The Return of Michael Myers
    c. Halloween 5: The Revenge of Michael Myers
    d. Halloween H20: 20 Years Later

81. What was the name of the grave keeper that showed Dr. Loomis the missing tombstone of Judith Myers?
    a. Derek Allen   c. Jack Kendall
    b. Taylor Madison   d. Chester Chesterfield

82. What character did Rob Zombie's wife portray?
    a. Annie Brackett   c. Judith Myers
    b. Laurie Strode   d. Deborah Myers

83. When at Smith's Grove Sanitarium, what did Michael say his favorite color was?
    a. White   c. Black
    b. Red   d. Blue

84. When Michael's pet died, what did he say he had to do?
    a. Bury Him   c. Flush Him
    b. Resurrect Him   d. Eat Him

85. Who played the roles of Mason and Cynthia Strode?
    a. Richmond Arquette and Sybil Danning
    b. Pat Skipper and Dee Wallace
    c. William Forsythe and Sheri Moon Zombie
    d. Clint Howard and Linda Sypien

86. When Michael first came downstairs, what did Ronnie say to him?
    a. Hello Michelle my bell
    b. Hello Michael my cycle
    c. Hello Killer my miller
    d. Hello Mikey my Dikey

87. What did Judith ask Michael she did to his pet when he announced it died?
    a. Stroke it to death   c. Bore it to death
    b. Feed it to death   d. Stab it to death

88. When Wesley saw Michael come out of the bathroom stall, what did he call him?
    a. Shitpants   c. Shitface
    b. Shithead   d. Shitsticks

89. What is the principal's first name?
    a. John   c. Jason
    b. Jim   d. Jarod

90. In the original *Halloween*, Michael strangled Lynda with a telephone cord. In this version of
Halloween, how does Michael strangle Lynda?
    a. Television Cable   c. Rope
    b. Electric Cord   d. His Bare Hands

91. What did the principal find in Michael's schoolbag?
    a. Pictures of him cutting himself
    b. Pictures of naked women
    c. Pictures of his weapons and masks
    d. Pictures of dead animals

92. What animal was also found dead in Michael's schoolbag wrapped in a plastic bag?
    a. A dead rat   c. A dead bird
    b. A dead dog   d. A dead cat

93. When Judith was eating cereal, what did Deborah say she was making for breakfast?
    a. Pancakes   c. Eggs
    b. French Toast   d. Toast

94. Where did the waitress Ronnie said was giving him the "freaky eye" work at?
    a. The Rabbit in Red   c. The Bingo Lounge
    b. The Haddonfield Diner   d. The Laugh Box

95. Lynda said her teacher in which class was flirting with her?
    a. Biology   c. English
    b. French   d. Math

96. Who played the role of Laurie Strode?
    a. Danielle Harris   c. Scout Taylor-Compton
    b. Kristina Klebe   d. Hanna R. Hall

97. What did Judith say eggs are?
    a. Chicken Feces   c. Chicken Abortions
    b. Chicken Embryos   d. Chicken Fetes

98. Who of the following did Lynda ask Laurie if he was flirting with her?
    a. Dr. Loomis   c. Bob Simms
    b. Paul Freedman   d. Sheriff Brackett

99. Nick Mennell played Bob Simms in *Halloween (2007)*. Who did he play in the other horror remake he starred in?
    a. Matt   c. Manny
    b. Maurice   d. Mike

100. Which two employees associated with Smith's Grove Sanitarium in the original *Halloween* film are absent from *Halloween (2007)*?
    a. Sam Loomis and Marion Chambers
    b. Sam Loomis and Terrence Wynn
    c. Marion Chambers and Terrence Wynn
    d. There was no absent employees in Halloween (2007)

Halloween 2 (2009)

1. Including Michael Myers, what was the body count of *Halloween 2 (2009)*?
    a. Nineteen
    b. Seventeen
    c. Eighteen
    d. Twenty

2. Who played Michael Myers in *Halloween 2 (2009)*?
    a. Brad Loree
    b. Christopher Durand
    c. Dick Warlock
    d. Tyler Mane

3. What was the budget of *Halloween 2 (2009)*?
    a. $13,000,000
    b. $11,000,000
    c. $14,000,000
    d. $15,000,000

4. Who directed *Halloween 2 (2009)*?
    a. John Carpenter
    b. Steve Miner
    c. Dwight H. Little
    d. Rob Zombie

5. When was *Halloween 2 (2009)* released into theaters?
    a. August 12, 2009
    b. August 24, 2009
    c. August 1, 2009
    d. August 28, 2009

6. What tattoo did Laurie have?
    a. A star with the letters "FTW"
    b. A moon with the letters "FTW"
    c. A sun with the letters "FTW"
    d. A jack-o'-lantern with the letters "FTW"

7. When Mya was calling 911, what did she say the address was of the Brackett household?
    a. 15 Cherrywood Road
    b. 31 Cherrywood Road
    c. 13 Cherrywood Road
    d. 7 Cherrywood Road

8. What did *Halloween 2 (2009)* make at the box office?
    a. $35.3 million
    b. $39.3 million
    c. $33.3 million
    d. $37.3 million

9. What type of car did Laurie have?
    a. Red Pontiac Firebird
    b. White Pontiac 3000 GT
    c. Blue Pontiac Grand Prix
    d. Orange Pontiac Sunfire

10. In the beginning, what music video was playing behind Laurie during her dream?
    a. Nights in White Satin by The Moody Blues
    b. Feel So Numb by Rob Zombie
    c. Thriller by Michael Jackson
    d. Smoke on the Water by Deep Purple

11. In the beginning of the film, what was the definition of a White Horse?
    a. Linked to instinct, purity, and the drive of the physical body to release powerful and emotional forces, like rage with ensuing damage and damnation.
    b. Linked to instinct, purity, and the drive of the physical body to release powerful and emotional forces, like rage with ensuing hellfire and brimstone.
    c. Linked to instinct, purity, and the drive of the physical body to release powerful and emotional forces, like rage with ensuing chaos and destruction.
    d. Linked to instinct, purity, and the drive of the physical body to release powerful and emotional forces, like rage with ensuing terror and fear.

12. What was the name of the talk show that Dr. Loomis appeared on?
    a. The Power Hour   c. The Newman Hour
    b. The Culture Shock   d. The Pop Show

13. Which rocker was featured on a poster in Laurie's bathroom?
    a. Rob Zombie   c. Ozzy Osbourne
    b. Metallica   d. Alice Cooper

14. What unusual request did Chett have for Dr. Loomis at the book signing?
    a. To Chett, The Bringer of Death, Johns
    b. To Chett, The Bringer of Life, Johns
    c. To Chett, The Bringer of Evil, Johns
    d. To Chett, The Bringer of Murder, Johns

15. When Laurie woke up in the hospital, which movie was playing on her television?
    a. Halloween 2 (1981)
    b. Night of the Living Dead
    c. Friday the 13th (1980)
    d. A Nightmare on Elm Street (1984)

16. What was the name of the coffee shop that Laurie worked at?
    a. Uncle Meat's Java Hole
    b. Uncle Meat's Java Hut
    c. Uncle Meat's Java Shoppe
    d. Uncle Meat's Java Club

17. According to a sign at the Rabbit in Red, what was Michael's nickname?
    a. The Legend of Haddonfield   c. The Butcher of Haddonfield
    b. The Myth of Haddonfield   d. The Psycho of Haddonfield

18. Which of the following is different from the original version of the film?
    a. In the original 1981 version of Halloween 2, Annie's corpse is discovered. In the 2009 version of Halloween 2, Annie's corpse isn't found.
    b. In the original 1981 version of Halloween 2, Annie isn't in the film. In the 2009 version of Halloween 2, Annie is in the film.
    c. In the original 1981 version of Halloween 2, Annie is already dead. In the 2009 version of Halloween 2, Annie is killed by Michael Myers.
    d. In the original 1981 version of Halloween 2, Annie is Sheriff Brackett's daughter. In the 2009 version of Halloween 2, Annie is Dr. Loomis' daughter.

19. What is the name of Dr. Loomis' new book?
    a. The Evil Returned to Haddonfield
    b. The Legend of Michael Myers
    c. The Devil Walks Among Us
    d. The Curse Known As Michael Myers

20. Who was also a guest on the talk show and embarrassed Dr. Loomis?
    a. Weird Al Yankovic
    b. Bubba the Love Sponge
    c. Howard Stern
    d. Regis Philbin

21. Who showed up to Dr. Loomis' book signing with a gun?
    a. The father of Paul Freedman
    b. The father of Lynda Van Der Klok
    c. The father of Bob Simms
    d. The father of Steve Haley

22. Who replaced Daeg Faerch as Young Michael Myers?
    a. Chase Wright Vanek
    b. Angus T. Jones
    c. Skyler Gisondo
    d. Preston Bailey

23. One year after the events from *Halloween (2007)*, who is Laurie living with?
    a. The Brackett's
    b. The Rockwell's
    c. The David's
    d. The Doyle's

24. This is the first film in the *Halloween* franchise that Michael does what as an adult?
    a. Gets Naked
    b. Dies
    c. Speaks
    d. Both B and C

25. Whose picture does Laurie have over her bed?
    a. Drew Peterson
    b. Charles Manson
    c. Scott Peterson
    d. The Zodiac Killer

26. How many calories of sugar did Annie say the pastry Sheriff Brackett was going to get had?
    a. 300 Calories
    b. 400 Calories
    c. 500 Calories
    d. 600 Calories

27. What was Annie making for breakfast?
    a. Egg Whites
    b. Turkey Bacon
    c. Jelly Toast
    d. Sausage

28. What did Sheriff Brackett say he was going to get on the way to the station?
    a. Marble Rye
    b. Bagel
    c. Boston Cream Donut
    d. Sticky Buns

29. Who played the role of Harley David?
    a. Angela Trimbur
    b. Scout Taylor-Compton
    c. Brea Grant
    d. Danielle Harris

30. What was Lou Martini dressed as for Halloween?
    a. Dracula
    b. Mummy
    c. Wolfman
    d. Frankenstein

31. In the beginning of the film, when defining a White Horse, which book was that an excerpt from?
    a. The Subconscious Nature of Nightmares
    b. The Subconscious Drive of Pattern Nightmares
    c. The Subconscious Psychosis of Dreams
    d. The Subconscious Psychological Understanding of Dreams

32. What was the name of Laurie's psychiatrist?
    a. Dr. Benita McCoy
    b. Dr. Billie McGinley
    c. Dr. Barbara Collier
    d. Dr. Bea Canterbury

33. What was the name of the owner of the Rabbit in Red?
    a. Howard Boggs
    b. Lou Martini
    c. Misty Dawn
    d. Sherman Benny

34. What was the first name of Lynda's dad?
    a. Karl
    b. Kyle
    c. Kory
    d. Keith

35. What were the names of the three people Michael killed, along with their dog, that were driving in a pickup truck at night?
    a. Sherman Benny, Jazlean Benny, and Frank
    b. Sherman Benny, Jazlean Benny, and Freud
    c. Sherman Benny, Jazlean Benny, and Floyd
    d. Sherman Benny, Jazlean Benny, and Fred

36. What was the name of the talk show host that interviewed Dr. Loomis?
    a. David Newman
    b. Derrien Newman
    c. Daniel Newman
    d. Darryl Newman

37. What was the name of the night watchman at the hospital in Laurie's dream?
    a. Bobby   c. Buddy
    b. Barry   d. Billy

38. What is Laurie's actual first name?
    a. Angie   c. Andi
    b. Angel   d. Amy

39. What was the name of the driver that stopped to help Laurie but was ultimately killed by Michael Myers?
    a. Brett   c. Becks
    b. Baron   d. Bobby

40. Laurie's psychiatrist said that the print in the picture hanging on her wall prompted ambiguous stimuli in the brain to form a picture. What did Laurie see in the picture?
    a. One White Horse   c. Three White Horses
    b. Two White Horses   d. Four White Horses

41. What was the name of the news reporter who interviewed Dr. Loomis about his book outside of the Myers house?
    a. Jazlean Benny   c. Wendy Snow
    b. Misty Dawn   d. Jane Salvador

42. What animal caused a car accident for the ambulance Michael Myers was in?
    a. Deer   c. Cow
    b. Horse   d. Elephant

43. After the events of the first film, *Halloween (2007)*, what did Laurie suffer from?
    a. Multiple Personality Disorder   c. Bipolar Disorder
    b. Post-Traumatic Stress Disorder   d. Attention Deficit Disorder

44. Who played the role of Wolfie?
    a. Chris Hardwick   c. Matt Bush
    b. Daniel Roebuck   d. Adam Boyer

45. What was the name of the deputy that Sheriff Brackett had watching over Annie?
    a. Deputy Andy Neale   c. Deputy Webb
    b. Deputy Lyons   d. Deputy Fred King

46. What literature character did the actor Justin Welborn dress as for Halloween in *Halloween 2 (2009)*?
    a. Dr. Jekyll   c. Mr. Hyde
    b. Tom Sawyer   d. Huckleberry Finn

47. In her dream, who does Laurie kill?
    a. Sheriff Brackett   c. Annie Brackett
    b. Dr. Loomis   d. Mya Rockwell

48. When Laurie told her psychiatrist that she walked through a park and saw this farm, what did she say this lady let her hold?
    a. Goat   c. Chicken
    b. Pig   d. Rooster

49. What did Laurie's psychiatrist say she'd give her to hold her over?
    a. Concerta   c. Lexapro
    b. Ritalin   d. Haldol

50. The medicine that Laurie's psychiatrist said she was going to give to her was what type of medication?
    a. Antipsychotic   c. Antidepressant
    b. Antihypertensive   d. Anticholinergic

51. What song played at the end of the film?
    a. Love Hurts   c. Mr. Sandman
    b. Teenage Frankenstein   d. Love is a Lie

52. On the sign at the Rabbit in Red, who was photographed in the picture as a way of advertising?
    a. Deborah Voorhees   c. Laurie Strode
    b. Annie Brackett   d. Judith Myers

53. What name did Lou Martini go by?
    a. Bad Lou   c. Bitchy Lou
    b. Baby Lou   d. Big Lou

54. Who was interviewing Lou Martini when he was dressed as Frankenstein?
    a. Holly West   c. Harriet West
    b. Helen West   d. Hillary West

55. Who played the role of Nurse Daniels?
    a. Viola Davis   c. Octavia Spencer
    b. Oprah Winfrey   d. Mary Birdsong

56. Lou's riddle to Howard was the following "What does a stripper do with her asshole before she dances?" What was the answer to his riddle?
    a. She gives him five bucks and tells him to take out the trash
    b. She gives him ten bucks and tells him to take out the trash
    c. She gives him two bucks and tells him to take out the trash
    d. She gives him twenty bucks and tells him to take out the trash

57. What was the temperature on the news Lou was watching?
    a. 49 Degrees   c. 45 Degrees
    b. 42 Degrees   d. 40 Degrees

58. On the sign at the bookstore where Dr. Loomis' books were being sold, what did it say about Michael Myers?
    a. He was born to kill   c. He was born to demolish
    b. He was born to destroy   d. He was born to massacre

59. On the sign promoting Dr. Loomis' book that Michael was looking at, what was the book's tagline listed above Dr. Loomis' head?
    a. The true story of America's most iconic serial murderer
    b. The true story of America's most legendary serial murderer
    c. The true story of America's most notorious serial murderer
    d. The true story of America's most mythological serial murderer

60. On the billboard promoting Dr. Loomis' book, what was the question being asked?
    a. Why am I alive?   c. Why am I here?
    b. Why am I killing?   d. Why am I famous?

61. When was Dr. Loomis' books set to hit the shelves in bookstores everywhere, according to his billboard?
    a. October 30th   c. October 31st
    b. October 25th   d. October 29th

62. What channel did Lou's interview air on?
    a. Channel 13 News   c. Channel 18 News
    b. Channel 21 News   d. Channel 6 News

63. Who played the role of Coroner Hooks?
    a. Richard Riehle   c. Howard Hesseman
    b. Dayton Callie   d. Duane Whitaker

64. What was the name of the stripper shown at the Rabbit in Red?
    a. Misty Dawn   c. Minnie Dearie
    b. Mimi Dynasty   d. Missy Dynamo

65. What was the name of the fan during Dr. Loomis' book signing?
    a. Chett Johns   c. Chett Jacobs
    b. Chett Jefferies   d. Chett James

66. Why did Chett say Michael Myers is different from the other serial killers?
    a. Because he eats at the center of the victim's soul
    b. Because he eats at the core of the victim's soul
    c. Because he eats at the vulnerable parts of the victim's soul
    d. Because he eats at the insecure parts of the victim's soul

67. What kind of crust did Annie tell her dad she wanted on the pizza?
    a. Thin Crust   c. Whole Wheat Crust
    b. Gluten Free Crust   d. Double Stuffed Crust

68. What did Sheriff Brackett respond to Annie with about the crust that she wanted to eat on the pizza?
    a. Why don't we just have them take the cheese and put it on cardboard
    b. Why don't we just have them take the cheese and put it on Styrofoam
    c. Why don't we just have them take the cheese and put it on aluminum foil
    d. Why don't we just have them take the cheese and put it on a sponge

69. What did Laurie say she didn't want on the pizza?
    a. Onions   c. Cheese
    b. Veggies   d. Meat

70. When Dr. Loomis was watching back his interview on The Newman Hour, the host sarcastically asked Dr. Loomis that there is no difference between Michael Myers and a what?
    a. Bear   c. Shark
    b. Dinosaur   d. Yeti

71. Who sings *Love Hurts* at the end of the film?
    a. Nan Verno   c. Nazareth
    b. The Cranberries   d. Cher

72. At the end of the film when Laurie is sitting in a white room, what does Deborah Voorhees have with her when walking toward Laurie?
    a. Black Dragon   c. White Horse
    b. Fiery Phoenix   d. Gold Lion

73. What was the word Michael Myers first spoke at the end of the film?
    a. Suffer   c. Rot
    b. Leave   d. Die

74. What color car does Laurie drive?
    a. Black   c. Orange
    b. White   d. Red

75. Who played the role of Gary Scott?
    a. Adam Boyer   c. Mark Boone Junior
    b. Jeff Daniel Phillips   d. Richard Brake

76. When Laurie was dreaming of killing Annie, what was she dressed as?
    a. A Clown   c. A Vampire
    b. A Witch   d. A Skeleton

77. What event from *Halloween (2007)* did Laurie imitate when she was dreaming of killing Annie?
    a. Michael Myers killing Judith Myers
    b. Michael Myers killing Steve Haley
    c. Michael Myers killing Ronnie White
    d. Michael Myers attacking the nurse at Smith's Grove Sanitarium

78. What was Chett's nickname?
    a. The Bringer of Death
    b. The Bringer of Life
    c. The Bringer of Evil
    d. The Bringer of Murder

79. Which two famous serial killers did Chett say Michael Myers is much better than?
    a. Jeffrey Dahmer and Charles Manson
    b. Jeffrey Dahmer and Ted Bundy
    c. Jeffrey Dahmer and OJ Simpson
    d. Jeffrey Dahmer and Drew Peterson

80. Who played the role of Barbara Collier?
    a. Margot Kidder   c. Mary Birdsong
    b. Betsy Rue   d. Caroline Williams

81. What was inside Kyle's copy of Dr. Loomis' book that he brought to the book signing?
    a. A picture of Michael Myers
    b. A picture of his daughter, Lynda
    c. A picture of Laurie
    d. A picture of his family together

82. Who did Harley David dress as for Halloween?
    a. A chick who is dressing up like a dude who wants to be a chick
    b. A dude who is dressing up like a chick who wants to be a dude
    c. A dude who is dressing up like a chick
    d. A chick who is dressing up like a dude

83. Laurie told which two people first about her being Michael Myers' sister?
    a. Annie Brackett and Sheriff Brackett
    b. Dr. Loomis and Sheriff Brackett
    c. Annie Brackett and Mya Rockwell
    d. Mya Rockwell and Harley David

84. What did the host of The Newman Hour say Dr. Loomis is infamous for when introducing him to the audience?
   a. For being the psychologist of America's leading serial killer
   b. For being the psychologist of America's most evil serial killer
   c. For being the psychologist of America's most vile serial killer
   d. For being the psychologist of America's famous serial killer

85. What was the question the host of The Newman Hour ask Dr. Loomis that Weird Al answered as a joke?
   a. You were criticized and outright accused of profiteering off the misery of others, how do you even respond to that criticism?
   b. You were criticized and outright accused of profiteering off the massacres that has happened, how do you even respond to that criticism?
   c. You were criticized and outright accused of profiteering off the misfortune of others, how do you even respond to that criticism?
   d. You were criticized and outright accused of profiteering off the heartbreak and agony that Michael has caused, how do you even respond to that criticism?

86. What was Dr. Loomis' answer to the above question after responding to Weird Al's sarcastic humor?
   a. Actually, I take great issue with that statement. Besides, I might say that I have endured quite a lot of pain and agony of my own in order to tell this story.
   b. Actually, I take great issue with that statement. Besides, I might say that I have endured quite a lot of misery of my own in order to tell this story.
   c. Actually, I take great issue with that statement. Besides, I might say that I have endured quite a lot of heartbreak of my own in order to tell this story.
   d. Actually, I take great issue with that statement. Besides, I might say that I have endured quite a lot of misfortune of my own in order to tell this story.

87. Where did Wolfie take Harley during the Halloween party to have sex?
   a. The Woods   c. His Truck
   b. A Barn   d. His Van

88. What did Wolfie name the answer to the above question?
   a. The Shagon Wagon   c. The Pimp Mobile
   b. The Hideout   d. The Truck Fuck

89. The host of the Halloween party told a joke. The joke was "What is the different between a Jack-o'-lantern and a blonde?" What was the answer?
   a. There is no difference. They both have a dumb expression and are hollow inside.
   b. There is no difference. They both have a perplexed expression and are hollow inside.
   c. There is no difference. They both have a blank expression and are hollow inside.
   d. There is no difference. They both have a dazed expression and are hollow inside.

90. When Laurie told Mya and Harley about being Michael's sister, what did Harley think Laurie was doing?
    a. Playing a Halloween trick   c. Joking
    b. Insane   d. Confused

91. What did Wolfie ask are real on Harley's body?
    a. Her boobs   c. Her tattoos
    b. Her hair   d. Her face

92. When Wolfie and Harley are having sex in the van, what song was playing in the background?
    a. I Just Want to Make Love to You by Foghat
    b. Love Hurts by Nana Vernon
    c. I Fell in Love by The Frank and Friends Big Band
    d. The Chase is Better than the Catch by Motorhead

93. What is the name of the band performing at the Halloween party?
    a. The Frank and Friends Big Band
    b. Motorhead
    c. Captain Clegg and the Night Creatures
    d. Diamond Head

94. When Wolfie said he had to pee, what did Harley respond with?
    a. Who said I don't want to watch?
    b. Who said I wasn't into watersports?
    c. Who said you can go pee?
    d. Who said you can just leave a girl alone in a van?

95. How did Laurie find out she is Michael Myers' sister?
    a. She heard Dr. Loomis tell Sheriff Brackett
    b. She read a note from her birth mother
    c. She saw it on the news
    d. She read it in Dr. Loomis' book

96. Who played the role of Nancy McDonald?
    a. Mary Birdsong   c. Nicky Whelan
    b. Sylvia Jefferies   d. Diana Ayala Goldner

97. When Laurie is being held down by Michael Myers as a kid, what did Dr. Loomis tell Laurie so she can fight it?
    a. It is all in her mind   c. It is all a hoax
    b. It is all make believe   d. It is all an illusion

98. What were Dr. Loomis' last words of the film?
    a. Michael, for God in Heaven
    b. Michael, don't let evil consume you
    c. Michael, think about what you're doing
    d. Michael, don't do this

99. Why was Laurie shot at the end of the film?
    a. Because she was helping Michael after being shot
    b. Because she had a gun
    c. Because she was reaching for Michael's knife
    d. Because she bent down next to Dr. Loomis

100. Who played the role of Mya Rockwell?
    a. Margot Kidder   c. Brea Grant
    b. Angela Trimbur   d. Nicky Whelan

Halloween (2018)

1. *Halloween (2018)* takes place how many years after the original events occurred?
    a. Twenty Years   c. Thirty Years
    b. Fifty Years   d. Forty Years

2. Which of the following films in the *Halloween* franchise does this film ignore in the storyline?
    a. Halloween 4 to 6
    b. Halloween 3
    c. Halloween 7 and 8
    d. All of them except the original

3. Which star from the original *Halloween* film returns in the leading role?
    a. Charles Cyphers   c. Kyle Richards
    b. Brian Andrews   d. Jamie Lee Curtis

4. Who directed *Halloween (2018)*?
    a. John Carpenter   c. Malek Akaad
    b. Danny McBride   d. David Gordon Green

5. What was the budget of *Halloween (2018)*?
    a. $5,000,000   c. $7,000,000
    b. $2,000,000   d. $10,000,000

6. Which past Michael Myers actor returns to don the mask again for only one scene with Jamie Lee Curtis, as well as the breathing sound effects during postproduction in *Halloween (2018)*?
    a. George P. Wilbur   c. Nick Castle
    b. Dick Warlock   d. Christopher Durand

7. Who portrays Michael Myers for a majority of the film, excluding the one scene with Jamie Lee Curtis?
    a. Omar J. Dorsey   c. Jefferson Hall
    b. James Jude Courtney   d. Toby Huss

8. What did *Halloween (2018)* make at the box office?
    a. $91.8 million   c. $91.4 million
    b. $91.1 million   d. $91.9 million

9. When was *Halloween (2018)* released into theaters?
    a. October 19, 2018   c. October 31, 2018
    b. October 30, 2018   d. October 23, 2018

10. Who portrayed Karen Strode?
    a. Judy Greer   c. Virginia Gardner
    b. Andi Matichak   d. Rhian Rees

11. Aaron Korey and Dana Haines had what job title?
    a. True-Crime British Journalists
    b. True-Crime British News Anchors
    c. True-Crime British Podcasters
    d. True-Crime British Meteorologists

12. Which actor/actress from the original *Halloween* film returned as the voice of the teacher?
    a. Nancy Loomis   c. PJ Soles
    b. Charles Cyphers   d. Kyle Richards

13. What was the name of the psychiatrist that took over for Dr. Sam Loomis when he died as Michael's psychiatrist?
    a. Dr. Cameron Elam   c. Dr. Frank Hawkins
    b. Dr. Ranbir Sartain   d. Dr. Aaron Korey

14. Who portrayed Vicky?
    a. Virginia Gardner   c. Judy Greer
    b. Rhian Rees   d. Andi Matichak

15. Which of the following characters from the original *Halloween* film is Cameron's father?
    a. Lonnie Elam   c. Ben Tramer
    b. Tommy Doyle   d. Bob Simms

16. What was the name of the boy that Vicky was babysitting?
    a. James   c. Julian
    b. Josiah   d. Jarrod

17. What was the working production title on set for the film?
    a. Uncle Black Cat   c. Uncle Witch
    b. Uncle Orange   d. Uncle Pumpkin

18. Which of the following from the original timeline is no longer in effect in this film?
    a. Michael killed his sister Judith
    b. Michael's psychiatrist was Dr. Sam Loomis
    c. Michael and Laurie are siblings
    d. Michael kills on Halloween

19. Which of the following *Halloween* films had an identical bus crash to this film?
    a. Halloween 5: The Revenge of Michael Myers
    b. Halloween: The Curse of Michael Myers
    c. Halloween: Resurrection
    d. Halloween 4: The Return of Michael Myers

20. What did Michael drop onto the floor in the stall that Dana Haines was using?
    a. Bloodied Fingernails   c. Bloodied Eyeballs
    b. Bloodied Teeth   d. Bloodied Hair

21. Who portrayed Sheriff Frank Hawkins?
    a. Will Patton
    b. Miles Robbins
    c. Jefferson Hall
    d. Drew Scheid

22. When did filming begin for *Halloween (2018)*?
    a. January 10, 2018
    b. January 4, 2018
    c. January 13, 2018
    d. January 21, 2018

23. Which two actresses were in talks of portraying Allyson?
    a. Abigail Breslin and Billie Lourd
    b. Scout-Taylor Compton and Danielle Harris
    c. Emma Roberts and Lucy Hale
    d. Carlson Young and Willa Fitzgerald

24. Among Aaron's collected files on Michael Myers was an illustration of whom?
    a. Annie Brackett
    b. Michael Myers as a boy
    c. Dr. Sam Loomis
    d. Marion Chambers

25. When Oscar sees Michael Myers, who does he call him in reference to *Halloween 2 (1981)*?
    a. Gary Hunt
    b. Jimmy
    c. Mr. Elrod
    d. Ben Tramer

26. What did Roth Cornet nickname the movie after watching the first trailer?
    a. Friday the 31st
    b. Grambo
    c. Samhain
    d. The Babysitter Murders

27. In Julian's bedroom, what was featured on the rotating lamp?
    a. Michael Myers' mask
    b. Rabbit in Red logo
    c. Clown with a knife
    d. Silver Shamrock Masks

28. What was the body count of *Halloween (2018)*?
    a. Eighteen
    b. Nineteen
    c. Twenty
    d. Twenty-One

29. Where did Ray say he accidentally got some peanut butter?
    a. The floor
    b. His penis
    c. The counter
    d. The dog bowl

30. After the end credits, what do you hear?
    a. Laurie's scream from the original film
    b. Michael breathing through his mask
    c. Dr. Sam Loomis' screams from parts 4 and 6
    d. Silver Shamrock's commercial song

31. Whose corpse did Michael put under the bedsheet as a ghost, symbolizing his entrance to the bedroom before he killed Lynda in *Halloween (1978)*?
    a. Dave
    b. Vicky
    c. Oscar
    d. Ray

32. What made Allyson pissed off at her boyfriend, Cameron?
    a. He was drunk and dirty dancing with three other girls at the dance
    b. He was drunk and passed out
    c. He was drunk and verbally abusing her
    d. He was drunk and making out with another girl at the dance

33. How much money did Aaron and Dana give Laurie for their interview with her regarding Michael Myers?
    a. $2000
    b. $3000
    c. $4000
    d. $5000

34. Who convinced Jamie Lee Curtis to reprise her role in the film?
    a. Channing Tatum
    b. John Carpenter
    c. Oliver Hudson
    d. Jake Gyllenhaal

35. Who portrayed Cameron Elam?
    a. Dylan Arnold
    b. James Jude Courtney
    c. Drew Scheid
    d. Will Patton

36. Where does Michael recover his mask?
    a. The trunk of Aaron's car
    b. A bag inside the bathroom stall
    c. A room inside Smith's Grove Sanitarium
    d. The medical bag of his psychiatrist

37. Who was mentioned as first on the scene to arrest Michael Myers after he was shot six times by Dr. Loomis?
    a. Sheriff Frank Hawkins
    b. Sheriff Leigh Brackett
    c. Deputy Gary Hunt
    d. Sheriff Ben Meeker

38. What two men does the cemetery caretaker say is buried in another cemetery not far from the one she is at now?
    a. Michael Jackson and Prince
    b. Abraham Lincoln and Edgar Allan Poe
    c. Patrick Swayze and Donald Pleasence
    d. Bernie Mac and Muddy Waters

39. Before Laurie is thrown off the balcony by Michael, Michael was hiding behind what before he jumped out to attack her?
    a. A rack of clothes
    b. A collection of Halloween masks
    c. A gun rack
    d. Mannequins

40. Where did Laurie tell Allyson she can go with the money to be safe?
    a. Canada   c. Europe
    b. Mexico   d. Hawaii

41. Why did Laurie break into Ray and Karen's house?
    a. To tell them about Michael's escape
    b. To tell them about her story 40 years ago
    c. To demonstrate the lack of security their house has
    d. To show them how much she actually loves them

42. Who portrayed Oscar?
    a. Drew Scheid   c. Dylan Arnold
    b. Toby Huss   d. Jefferson Hall

43. At the end of the film, who is holding the knife in the back of the pickup truck?
    a. Laurie Strode   c. Karen Strode
    b. Allyson   d. None of the Above

44. When Michael is being engulfed in flames at the end of the film, what is particularly
noticeable after Laurie leaves the burning house?
    a. Michael is screaming in pain and agony
    b. Michael is trying to climb out of the room he was trapped in
    c. Michael takes off his mask
    d. Michael has disappeared from the room he was in when the house was set on fire

45. How does Laurie become aware of Michael's whereabouts when she was patrolling the
streets in her truck?
    a. She saw Michael's shadow walking behind a house
    b. Sheriff Frank Hawkins told Laurie that Michael was seen heading towards her daughter's
    house
    c. She remembered that he goes after babysitters on Halloween night and remembered that
    Allyson's best friend, Vicky, was babysitting a kid named Julian
    d. She heard a dispatch call on her truck's CB radio after Julian fled the house where Michael
    was attacking Vicky and called 911

46. How does Allyson attempt to trick Dr. Sartain in letting her go?
    a. She said that Michael is starting to wake up
    b. She said that she knows why Michael is evil and intended on killing her grandmother
    c. She said that Dr. Loomis has files in her grandmother's house that she can get him
    d. She said that Michael spoke to her

47. What is the name of Cameron's best friend?
    a. Oscar   c. Dave
    b. Allyson   d. Vicky

48. Who portrayed Dave?
    a. Toby Huss
    b. Jibrail Nantambu
    c. Dylan Arnold
    d. Miles Robbins

49. Why were Aaron and Dana so interested in Michael Myers?
    a. They wanted to see why he committed the murders in 1978
    b. They wanted to see what was possessing him to be evil
    c. They wanted to know more about why the Cult of Thorn drives him to kill
    d. They wanted to know if he really heard a voice the night he killed his sister, Judith

50. What was the date of birth on Judith's tombstone?
    a. November 10, 1947
    b. November 5, 1947
    c. November 15, 1947
    d. November 25, 1947

51. Before Michael breaks into a lady's house to retrieve his signature kitchen knife, what does he kill her with?
    a. Screwdriver
    b. Saw
    c. Hammer
    d. Nail Gun

52. Regarding question 51, what in particular does this lady have that is made evident after her death?
    a. She has a newborn baby
    b. She is pregnant due to a positive pregnancy test
    c. She is a newlywed
    d. She is a widow

53. Which of the following is not something Laurie did in *Halloween (2018)* that Michael originally did in *Halloween (1978)*?
    a. Laurie broke into a closet to attack Michael
    b. Laurie fell off a balcony and landed onto the grass, as Michael looked over the balcony, Laurie was gone
    c. Laurie lurked in the shadows and attacked Michael when he didn't expect it or see her
    d. Laurie was standing outside of the schoolhouse and Allyson saw Laurie standing there and watching her while she was in class

54. What did Laurie do every night for forty years and why did she do it?
    a. She trained every night, so she can be prepared for Michael when he comes for her
    b. She meditated every night, so she was mentally prepared for her final battle with Michael
    c. She would build the fortress she currently lives in for extra protection against Michael
    d. She prayed every night that Michael would escape so she can kill him

55. Who portrayed Dana Haines?
    a. Rhian Rees
    b. Virginia Gardner
    c. Judy Greer
    d. Andi Matichak

56. Where did Vicky, Oscar, and Cameron all go to together?
    a. A Halloween Rave   c. A Halloween Dance
    b. A 40th Anniversary Halloween Party   d. A Halloween Satanic Ritual

57. What did Oscar do to Allyson before he was killed?
    a. Hugged her   c. Asked her on a date
    b. Kissed her   d. Asked to hookup

58. What did Laurie's trauma cost her in life?
    a. Her sanity and freedom
    b. Two marriages and custody of her daughter, Karen
    c. Three jobs
    d. Her friendship with Dr. Loomis

59. What was Ray doing in the kitchen?
    a. Cooking breakfast   c. Setting mousetraps
    b. Doing the dishes   d. Cleaning the countertops

60. Where is Laurie's "safe place" located at?
    a. In a hidden door behind her closet
    b. In a hidden bunker underneath her kitchen island
    c. In a hidden passage behind a bookcase
    d. In a hidden alcove under her bed

61. When Allyson is running through the woods, she comes across a bunch of mannequins and targets that was seen earlier in the film during which of the following scenes?
    a. When Laurie had her daughter training for the moment Michael would escape
    b. When Laurie was shooting her guns for practice in preparation for Michael's impending escape
    c. When Aaron and Dana were heading to Laurie's house to conduct an interview with her
    d. When Sheriff Frank Hawkins was patrolling the streets

62. When the bus crashed, who was wandering the streets?
    a. The doctors of Smith's Grove Sanitarium   c. The injured driver
    b. The patients of Smith's Grove Sanitarium   d. Michael Myers

63. Who portrayed Ray?
    a. Haluk Bilginer   c. Drew Scheid
    b. Will Patton   d. Toby Huss

64. Who kills Sheriff Frank Hawkins and kidnaps Michael to take him to Laurie?
    a. Officer Richards   c. Aaron Korey
    b. Dr. Ranbir Sartain   d. Warden Kuneman

65. When Michael breaks through the glass of the door and grabs Laurie, what does Laurie shoot to free herself from his grasp?
    a. His face
    b. His shoulder
    c. His chest
    d. His hand

66. How did Karen know which gun to use when Michael found the hidden bunker?
    a. Karen's initials were on the gun
    b. Karen remembered which gun she always practiced with as a child
    c. Laurie told Karen that it was the gun to use if Michael found her
    d. Karen intuitively just chose that gun

67. How does Aaron try to get Michael to speak at Smith's Grove Sanitarium?
    a. He mentioned the morbid details of how he killed his sister, Judith
    b. He mentioned how Dr. Sam Loomis tried to stop Michael from his killing spree
    c. He shows Michael the mask he wore and mentioned Laurie's name
    d. He explains the significance of Halloween and why Michael chose that day to kill his sister

68. Where does Laurie shoot Michael when she sees him in an upstairs window?
    a. His head
    b. His heart
    c. His stomach
    d. His shoulder

69. What does Karen shoot Michael with?
    a. A shotgun
    b. A rifle
    c. A pistol
    d. A machine gun

70. When Laurie found Ray's body on the closet shelf, which character's corpse from *Halloween (1978)* did it resemble?
    a. Annie Brackett
    b. Bob Simms
    c. Lynda Van Der Klok
    d. Judith Myers

71. While Laurie is hunting down Michael in her home, what does she do after leaving each room?
    a. Presses a button to barricade the room, so she knows she checked it and Michael is not in it
    b. Fires a warning shot into the wall to let Karen know where she is located, and Michael isn't there
    c. Grabs another weapon or more ammo to be prepared for the next room she is about to enter
    d. Rapidly shoots her gun in case Michael is hiding outside of the room she is leaving

72. Which television show and movie were playing on the television sets in *Halloween (2018)*?
    a. Voyagers and The Exorcist
    b. Voyagers and Repo Man
    c. Voyagers and The Thing
    d. Voyagers and Friday the 13th

73. Which of the following actors expressed interest in playing Michael Myers?
    a. Chris Evans   c. Jason Momoa
    b. Robert Downey Jr.   d. Leigh Whannell

74. What does Laurie stab Michael with to allow Karen and Allyson to escape?
    a. A knife   c. A cleaver
    b. A fireplace poker   d. A syringe

75. Who portrayed Dr. Ranbir Sartain?
    a. Jibrail Nantambu   c. Jefferson Hall
    b. Haluk Bilginer   d. Miles Robbins

76. What is the name of Vicky's boyfriend?
    a. Oscar   c. Cameron
    b. Dave   d. Julian

77. What does Dr. Ranbir Sartain tell Aaron and Dana about Michael at Smith's Grove Sanitarium?
    a. He is planning his escape
    b. He is recovering from the six shots he received from Dr. Sam Loomis
    c. He can speak but refuses to do so
    d. He stares at the picture of Laurie Strode every day for hours

78. When Laurie discovers Michael Myers in an upstairs bedroom, who is noticeable from a past *Halloween* film roaming the streets?
    a. Trick-or-Treaters wearing Silver Shamrock Halloween masks
    b. Druids from the Cult of Thorn
    c. Patients from the Smith's Grove Sanitarium
    d. The Silver Shamrock Androids

79. How does Karen trap Michael in the safe room as it filled up with gas?
    a. By closing the passageway using the kitchen island
    b. By putting a heavy sofa to cover the safe room's entry/exit
    c. By flipping the switch and having the metal bars close the exit from the room
    d. By barricading the room's entry/exit with heavy furniture and equipment

80. Who portrayed Allyson?
    a. Andi Matichak   c. Rhian Rees
    b. Jamie Lee Curtis   d. Judy Greer

81. Where is Michael being transferred to?
    a. Smith's Grove Sanitarium's solitary confinement
    b. A state prison
    c. A mental institution
    d. A maximum security prison

82. When talking to Vicky on the phone, Allyson mentioned that Halloween is on a what?
   a. Weekend   c. School night
   b. Friday   d. Family game night

83. On the television, the newscaster is heard as describing the events of *Halloween (1978)* as what?
   a. The Haddonfield Slaughtering   c. The Halloween Massacre
   b. The Monster Mash   d. The Babysitter Murders

84. At Smith's Grove Sanitarium, which of the following indicates the most dangerous patients?
   a. Yellow-Lined Checkered Squares
   b. Black-Lined Checkered Squares
   c. Red-Lined Checkered Squares
   d. Blue-Lined Checkered Squares

85. While the father and his son are driving and before they see the crashed bus, the son tells his father he enjoys his what?
   a. Halloween costume   c. X-Box One
   b. New Bedroom   d. Dance Classes

86. What is the address of the disturbance that came across the police band?
   a. 707 Meridian   c. 15 Lampkin
   b. 1428 Elm   d. 21 Dayta

87. Who portrayed Aaron Korey?
   a. Nick Castle   c. Jefferson Hall
   b. James Jude Courtney   d. Toby Huss

88. What does Laurie say to Michael when she sets him on fire in the safe room?
   a. Happy Halloween, Michael   c. Burn in Hell, Michael
   b. Trick-or-Treat, Michael   d. Rest in Peace, Michael

89. What does Allyson say to Vicky regarding Michael being Laurie's brother?
   a. It was a rumor that circulated for a while but was found to be untrue
   b. It was true until a DNA test proved otherwise
   c. It was a bad storyline that people told when discussing the murders
   d. It was a story that people just made up

90. What was Michael trying to do to Laurie when he smashed through her door
   a. Break her neck   c. Take her gun away
   b. Break down the door to gain access to her home   d. Strangle her to death

91. On which of the follow dates did Jamie Lee Curtis announce via Twitter that she was returning to play Laurie Strode?
   a. September 19, 2017   c. September 9, 2017
   b. September 15, 2017   d. September 17, 2017

92. Which of the following were the original working titles for *Halloween (2018)*?
    a. Halloween Returns and Halloween: The Origin of Michael Myers
    b. Halloween Returns and Halloween: The Shape of Michael Myers
    c. Halloween Returns and Halloween H40: 40 Years Later
    d. Halloween Returns and Halloween: The Evil of Michael Myers

93. The gas station is the same, exact replica as the gas station in which previous *Halloween* film?
    a. Halloween 3: Season of the Witch
    b. Halloween 4: The Return of Michael Myers
    c. Halloween 5: The Revenge of Michael Myers
    d. Halloween H20: 20 Years Later

94. Who portrayed Julian?
    a. Rhian Rees   c. Jefferson Hall
    b. Haluk Bilginer   d. Jibrail Nantambu

95. What does Aaron and Dana ask Laurie to do with Michael?
    a. Meet with him as a last attempt to get him to speak
    b. Meet with him and see if his rage occurs again
    c. Meet with him and see if there is a pattern in his attack on her like there was with Judith
    d. Meet with him and see if she can make a connection with him

96. Why can't Karen and Ray get in contact with Allyson?
    a. Because her phone died
    b. Because Cameron put her phone in food causing it to malfunction
    c. Because she forgot her phone at the Halloween dance
    d. Because she dropped her phone when she was running after seeing Oscar's dead body

97. What was the date of death on Judith's tombstone?
    a. October 31, 1957   c. October 31, 1978
    b. October 31, 1972   d. October 31, 1963

98. Danny McBride, when appearing on Empire Film Podcast to promote *Alien: Covenant*, was jokingly asked if he'd be playing Michael Myers due to his large build, to which Danny responded by saying what?
    a. Oh God no! Michael's supposed to be a terrifying creeper with good posture, not Peter Griffin!
    b. Oh God no! Michael's supposed to be a terrifying creeper with good posture, not Homer Simpson!
    c. Oh God no! Michael's supposed to be a terrifying creeper with good posture, not Elmer Fudd!
    d. Oh God no! Michael's supposed to be a terrifying creeper with good posture, not Winnie the Pooh!

99. Who portrayed Laurie Strode?
    a. PJ Soles   c. Judy Greer
    b. Jamie Lee Curtis   d. Scout-Taylor Compton

100. What has Laurie been dealing with for the past forty years?
    a. Post-Traumatic Stress Disorder   c. Multiple Personality Disorder
    b. Schizophrenia   d. Drug Addiction

Halloween Mashup

Part 1: Word Scramble

Unscramble the following *Halloween* words, terms, or characters.

1. CRMSAE NEUEQ ________________ ______________
2. OEIDHLDNDAF ______________________
3. ROTNH ________________
4. LLOEWHEAN __________________
5. MCLHIEA SMRYE ________________ ____________
6. LEIV ______________
7. VESIRL HKCRSOAM ________________ ______________
8. CHTBUER NIKEF ______________ ____________
9. BBRIAT NI DRE ____________ ______ __________
10. DTTMAAENRRNIGNEN ______________________
11. TOBCORE ________________
12. OONBMYEGAM __________________
13. YITBASTBIIGN __________________
14. HET PSEHA ____________ ______________
15. ETH NIICCL ______________ ______________

Part 2: Who Am I?

16. I am the niece of a serial killer. I survived my first two ordeals with him, but later was killed after giving birth. I tried to protect my baby after foreseeing my death and hid him well. Who am I? ______________________

17. I am a mother who loved her son. I couldn't believe he killed Ronnie, Judith, and Judith's boyfriend in cold blood. I worked as a stripped at the Rabbit in Red. After my son was locked up and I figured there'd be no way to protect him, I put a bullet in my head while watching a slideshow of him as a boy. Who am I? ______________________

18. I am the brother of a real estate owner and took over his company. I also bought the Myers House for my family to live in at a very cheap price without telling them and am the reason they got butchered by Michael. I tend to be a jackass and come off as an asshole to my family. I don't believe in the Boogeyman, but found out the hard way that he exists. Who am I?

____

19. I am the head nurse at Haddonfield Memorial Hospital. I tend to be a bit of a prude, but I am just doing my job. I kept checking on Laurie Strode after she was brutally attacked by Michael Myers. I also yelled at Nurse Karen Bailey. Who am I? ______________________

20. I am the owner of the factory called Silver Shamrock. I make Halloween masks and plan to use my "innovation" to kill children worldwide. I got rich off cheap gags and Halloween masks. I also am an Irishman. Who am I? ___________________________

21. We are a dysfunctional family. We consist of the father, Buddy, the mother, Betty, and our son, Buddy Jr. We are looking to refill our purchase order of the Silver Shamrock masks. We all died as a family during the demonstration to Dr. Challis on how these masks plan on killing children worldwide when they wear them during the giveaway. Who are we?

____

22. I am the annoying best friend of Rachel. I went to the Tower Farms Halloween party despite being told my life was in danger. I'm close to Jamie and sacrificed my own life to protect hers. Who am I? ___________________________

23. I am the stepmother of Jamie and mother of Rachel. I went out on Halloween night to my husband's work dinner. I got home and Rachel and Jamie weren't home before curfew. I later found out why and when getting Jamie ready for her bath, I was stabbed with a pair of scissors. I did survive the ordeal. Who am I? ___________________________

24. I am the reason Michael escaped from Smith's Grove Sanitarium. I also kidnapped Jamie and broke Michael out of the jail cell. I work at Smith's Grove Sanitarium and control Michael with the Curse of Thorn. I also taught Michael how to drive. Who am I? ___________________________

25. I am Rachel's love interest. I got mad that Rachel blew me off and went out with Kelly Meeker, the sheriff's daughter. I later tried to make it up to Rachel by protecting her but I failed. I also work at the Discount Mart. Who am I? ___________________________

26. I am evil. I have the eyes of the devil per my psychiatrist. I am provoked by the Curse of Thorn. As a kid, I killed my sister and was locked up. Now, I am wanting to kill my other sister, Laurie. Who am I? ___________________________

27. I babysat Michael on Halloween in 1963 when he killed his sister in cold blood. I am a member of the cult that rages Michael into a killing machine. Who am I? ___________________________

28. I always use the word "totally". I am a cheerleader and best friends with Laurie and Annie. I am also dating Bob. Who am I? ___________________________

29. I was looking after Michael for years after both he and Dr. Loomis burned to death. I then handed him over to the state. I then told Dr. Loomis about an ambulance accident and followed him to the scene for the crash. Who am I? ___________________________

30. I am not a real person as I was in someone's dream. I worked at the hospital and drove a truck. I got an axe in my back in front of this young, scared girl named Laurie. Who am I? ____________________

Part 3: Fill in the Blank

31. What was the type of dance that Laurie, Annie, and Lynda were going to go to? ____________________

32. What was the name of Rachel and Jamie's dog in Halloween 4: The Return of Michael Myers? ________________

33. Who was the actor that the Michael Myers mask was molded from? ____________________

34. What was the name of Lindsay's dog in Halloween (1978)? ________________

35. What was the name of Rachel's dog in Halloween 5: The Revenge of Michael Myers? ______________

36. What did Mr. Elrod decline on his sandwich in Halloween 2 (1981)? ____________________

37. What did Michael use to kill Wesley in Halloween (2007)? ______________

38. What year did Michael kill his sister as a boy? ____________

39. What state is Haddonfield located in? __________________

40. In the production cut of Halloween 6: The Curse of Michael Myers, whose baby was Michael the father of? __________________

41. What was sticking out of Dr. Mixter's eye in Halloween 2 (1981)? __________________

42. The Halloween theme song was created by John Carpenter on what instrument? __________

43. What color was Rachel's robe in Halloween 5: The Revenge of Michael Myers? _________

44. What was Samantha Thomas dressed as for the Halloween party? __________________

45. Besides Freddie, who helped Sara survive Michael Myers? ________________

Part 4: Hidden Character

Find the hidden character by filling in the quotes below. Once completed, the bubbles will spell out the hidden character.

46. That was the _ _ _ _ _ _ O _ _.
47. Behind that boy's eyes was purely and simply _ _ O _.
48. You're looking a little O _ _ _ _ _ there Mikey.
49. I'll see you in O _ _ _.
50. Trick or _ _ _ O _.
51. The only bastard I see in this _ _ _ O is you.
52. He was doing very well last night. Maybe someone around here gave him O _ _ _ _ _ _.
53. He's come _ _ O _.
54. Both of them _ _ _ _ _ O burned to death.
55. _ _ _ _ O ' _ an orphan.
56. Death has come to your little town, _ _ _ O _ _ _.
57. It's Halloween. Everyone is entitled to one good O _ _ _ _.

Hidden Character: _______________________ ______________

Part 5: True or False

58. Deborah Voorhees was the stepmother of Michael Myers.
     a. True   b. False

59. Laurie Strode is the adopted daughter of John and Debra Strode.
     a. True   b. False

60. Harley dressed as a dude who wants to be a chick for Halloween?
     a. True   b. False

61. Josh Hartnett, who played John Tate, also starred in the movie Pearl Harbor?
     a. True   b. False

62. Skyler Gisondo, who played Tommy Doyle in Halloween (2007), had a role in season 3 of Once Upon a Time as Devin?
     a. True   b. False

63. Before discovering Samantha and Spitz's corpses, Tina saw a cat with blood on its fur?
     a. True   b. False

64. Mike in Halloween 5: The Revenge of Michael Myers was driving a Dodge Viper?
     a. True   b. False

65. Dr. Loomis survived the explosion with Michael Myers at the end of Halloween 2 (1981)?
    a. True   b. False

Part 6: This or That

66. Michael Myers killed his sister or his brother?
    a. His Sister   b. His Brother

67. Michael Myers is evil or holy?
    a. Evil   b. Holy

68. Michael Myers wrote on the chalkboard in Halloween 2 the word Halloween or Samhain?
    a. Halloween   b. Samhain

69. Per Dr. Loomis, Samhain means Day of the Dead or All Hallows' Eve?
    a. Day of the Dead   b. All Hallows' Eve

70. Laurie Strode is the original final girl or the original victim?
    a. Original Final Girl   b. Original Victim

71. Lester only hates Lynda or only hates Annie?
    a. Lynda   b. Annie

72. Conal Cochran is from Scotland or Ireland?
    a. Scotland   b. Ireland

73. Jamie Lee Curtis, who plays Laurie Strode, is a true Scream Queen or a true Kill Machine?
    a. Scream Queen   b. Kill Machine

74. Will is the boarding school's principal or guidance counselor?
    a. Principal   b. Guidance Counselor

75. The boarding school's class trip was to Yellowstone National Park or Yosemite National Park?
    a. Yellowstone National Park   b. Yosemite National Park

76. In Halloween H20: 20 Years Later, Laurie Strode/Keri Tate liked drinking merlot or chardonnay?
    a. Merlot   b. Chardonnay

77. Deckard is a high school student or a college student?
    a. High School Student   b. College Student

78. Dr. Mixter goes to a country club or a strip club?
    a. Country Club   b. Strip Club

79. Nurse Karen Bailey is always on time or always late?
    a. Always on time   b. Always late

80. By the end of the Halloween franchise, Laurie Strode survives or dies?
    a. Survives   b. Dies

Part 7: Matching

Match the actor/actress to the character he/she played by putting the correct letter on the line.

81. Nancy Stephens ___	a. Sheriff Ben Meeker
82. PJ Soles ___	b. Marion Chambers
83. Nancy Kyes ___	c. Jimmy
84. Hunter Von Leer ___	d. Dr. Sam Loomis
85. Beau Starr ___	e. Michael Myers
86. Wendi Kaplan ___	f. Annie Brackett
87. Donald Pleasence ___	g. Freddie Harris
88. Busta Rhymes ___	h. Lynda Van Der Klok
89. George P. Wilbur ___	i. Deputy Gary Hunt
90. Lance Guest ___	j. Tina Williams

Part 8: Who Said It?

Put on the line who said each of the listed quotes.

91. "You can't have the baby, Michael!" _______________
92. "They're all going to kill us!" _______________________
93. "Yeah. I'm fine baby. The bullet just grazed me!" _______________
94. "It's almost time to come home, Angel!" _____________________________
95. "I bet she wears crotchless panties and barks like a dog!" _______________
96. "Hello, dear!" ___________________
97. "Leigh, they found three bodies. Across from the Doyle house. Three kids. Leigh, one of them was Annie!" __________________
98. "I'm getting my nipples pierced" _________________
99. "Michael Myers, get your ass over here" __________________
100. "Fuck off, Wade" _________________

Part 9: Who Played Who?

Next to each character, write the actor's name.

101. Who played Rachel Carruthers? ___________________
102. Who played Samantha Thomas? ___________________
103. Who played Ellie Grimbridge? ___________________
104. Who played John Tate? ___________________
105. Who played Brady? ___________________
106. Who played Nurse Jill Franco? ___________________
107. Who played Becks? ___________________
108. Who played Danny Strode? ___________________
109. Who played Will Brennan? ___________________
110. Who played Kelly Meeker? ___________________
111. Who played Rudy Grimes? ___________________
112. Who played Mrs. Alves? ___________________
113. Who played Billy Hill? ___________________
114. Who played Dr. Hoffman? ___________________
115. Who played Wolfie? ___________________
116. Who played Nora Winston? ___________________
117. Who played Dr. Terrence Wynn? ___________________
118. Who played Alice Martin? ___________________
119. Who played Lonnie Elam? ___________________
120. Who played Kyle Van Der Klok? ___________________
121. Who played Jenna Danzig? ___________________
122. Who played Norma Watson? ___________________
123. Who played Ismael Cruz? ___________________
124. Who played Nurse Mary? ___________________
125. Who played Tim Strode? ___________________
126. Who played John Strode? ___________________
127. Who played Marge Guttman? ___________________
128. Who played Spitz? ___________________
129. Who played Linda Challis? ___________________
130. Who played Budd Scarlotti? ___________________
131. Who played Mrs. Elrod? ___________________
132. Who played Jackson Sayer? ___________________
133. Who played Dr. Frederick Mixter? ___________________
134. Who played Mrs. Blankenship? ___________________
135. Who played Deputy Logan? ___________________
136. Who played Marshal Terrence Gummell? ___________________
137. Who played Jimmy Howell? ___________________
138. Who played Nurse Janet Marshall? ___________________
139. Who played Aron? ___________________
140. Who played Debra Strode? ___________________
141. Who played Kara Strode? ___________________
142. Who played Nurse Karen Bailey? ___________________

143. Who played Deckard? ___________________
144. Who played Starker? ___________________
145. Who played Teddy? ___________________
146. Who played Nurse Agnes? ___________________
147. Who played Uncle Meat? ___________________
148. Who played Paul Freedman? ___________________
149. Who played Nurse Daniels? ___________________
150. Who played Darlene Carruthers? ___________________

Part 10: Multiple Choice

151. Which dream film was always being discussed about Michael Myers in a crossover, but is just rumors and may never happen?
    a. Michael vs. Freddy   c. Michael vs. Jason
    b. Michael vs. Pinhead   d. Michael vs. Ghostface

152. Which of the *Halloween* films did Jamie Lee Curtis star in, either as a main star or a minor role?
    a. Halloween (1978), Halloween 2 (1981), Halloween 4: The Return of Michael Myers, Halloween H20: 20 Years Later, and Halloween: Resurrection
    b. Halloween (1978), Halloween 2 (1981), Halloween 6: The Curse of Michael Myers, Halloween H20: 20 Years Later, and Halloween: Resurrection
    c. Halloween (1978), Halloween 2 (1981), Halloween 3: Season of the Witch, Halloween H20: 20 Years Later, and Halloween: Resurrection
    d. Halloween (1978), Halloween 2 (1981), Halloween 5: The Revenge of Michael Myers, Halloween H20: 20 Years Later, and Halloween: Resurrection

153. What was the approximate budget of all the *Halloween* films combined?
    a. $72,350,000   c. $72,325,000
    b. $72,375,000   d. $72,300,000

154. What instrument was used to create the *Halloween 2 (1981)* theme song?
    a. Synthesizer Piano   c. Synthesizer Cello
    b. Synthesizer Violin   d. Synthesizer Organ

155. What was the original title for *Halloween (1978)*?
    a. The Babysitter Killers   c. The Babysitter Murders
    b. The Babysitter Stalkers   d. The Babysitter Obsession

156. What was the name of the *Halloween* documentary released on July 25, 2006?
    a. 20 Years of Terror   c. 30 Years of Terror
    b. 25 Years of Terror   d. 35 Years of Terror

157. Who narrated the above documentary?
    a. Nancy Kyes   c. Jamie Lee Curtis
    b. PJ Soles   d. Danielle Harris

158. Which slasher film inspired the creation of *Halloween (1978)*?
    a. Friday the 13th   c. The Texas Chainsaw Massacre
    b. A Nightmare on Elm Street   d. Psycho

159. In 1983, *Halloween* was released as a video game of which gaming console?
    a. NES   c. Atari
    b. Super Nintendo   d. Sega Genesis

160. Over a four-month period, who wrote a total of three young adult novels on *Halloween,* albeit unrelated to the films?
    a. Kelly O'Rourke   c. Curtis Richards
    b. Nicholas Grabowsky   d. Jack Martin

161. Where did the 25-year anniversary of *Halloween (1978)* convention take place?
    a. Pasadena, California   c. Los Angeles, California
    b. Anaheim, California   d. San Francisco, California

162. Which actor that played an iconic killer in a horror franchise was a guest speaker during the *Halloween* documentary?
    a. Kane Hodder   c. Robert Englund
    b. Brad Dourif   d. Clive Barker

163. On February 9, 2017, John Carpenter stated that the next *Halloween* film will be released on which date and be a direct sequel to *Halloween 2 (1981)*?
    a. October 31, 2018   c. October 30, 2018
    b. October 19, 2018   d. October 13, 2018

164. On February 9, 2017, John Carpenter said which of the following will be directing the next film in the *Halloween* franchise?
    a. Malek Akkad   c. Danny McBride
    b. David Gordon Green   d. Rob Zombie

165. Premiering on The Biography Channel on October 28, 2010, what was the name of the *Halloween* documentary?
    a. Halloween: The Inside Scoop
    b. Halloween: The Inside Story
    c. The Making of Halloween
    d. Halloween: The Original Slasher

166. What was the month and year of the 25th anniversary convention of *Halloween (1978)*?
    a. October 2005   c. October 2003
    b. October 2001   d. October 1999

167. *Halloween* is the 4th ranked grossing horror film franchise, with the Hannibal Lecter series being 3rd and *A Nightmare on Elm Street* being 2nd. Which film is the first ranked grossing horror film franchise?
    a. Scream
    b. Saw
    c. Friday the 13th
    d. The Texas Chainsaw Massacre

168. Who did John Carpenter receive help from in performing the *Halloween* theme song?
    a. Debra Hill
    b. Rob Zombie
    c. Dan Wyman
    d. Alice Cooper

169. Which instrument was used to create the theme song for *Halloween (1978)*?
    a. Organ
    b. Violin
    c. Piano
    d. Cello

170. Which previous film of John Carpenter's inspired Moustapha Akkad and Irwin Yablans to have John Carpenter write and direct *Halloween (1978)*?
    a. The Thing
    b. Assault on Precinct 13
    c. The Fog
    d. Dark Star

171. How many days did it take to film *Halloween (1978)*?
    a. 20 Days
    b. 18 Days
    c. 30 Days
    d. 21 Days

172. The first *Halloween* comic book was simply titled *Halloween*. What was the first sequel titled?
    a. Halloween: The Blackest Eyes
    b. Halloween: The Devil's Eyes
    c. Halloween: The Origin of Michael Myers
    d. Halloween: The Devil Walks Among Us

173. The first *Halloween* comic book was simply titled *Halloween*. What was the second sequel titled?
    a. Halloween: The Origin of Michael Myers
    b. Halloween: The Blackest Eyes
    c. Halloween: The Devil Walks Among Us
    d. Halloween: The Devil's Eyes

174. What was the approximately amount of box office sales for the *Halloween* franchise only in the United States?
    a. $308,189,322
    b. $308,774,929
    c. $308,824,329
    d. $308,522,645

175. What was the name of the first *Halloween*-related book, yet unrelated to the film's timeline, that was released on October 1, 1997?
    a. The Scream Queen
    b. The Scream Demon
    c. The Scream Factory
    d. The Scream of Death

176. In the novelization of the *Halloween (1978)* film, what two things did the novel expand on?
  a. The festival of Samhain and the legend of Michael Myers
  b. The festival of Samhain and Michael's time at the sanitarium
  c. The festival of Samhain and Michael's childhood
  d. The festival of Samhain and the history of Halloween

177. Who wrote the novelization of the *Halloween (1978)* film?
  a. Nicholas Grabowsky   c. Jack Martin
  b. Kelly O'Rourke   d. Curtis Richards

178. How much did all the *Halloween* films approximately make in the box office combined?
  a. $396,122,771   c. $396,122,778
  b. $396,122,773   d. $396,122,377

179. In the novelization of the *Halloween 2 (1981)* film, what was added to the novel?
  a. An additional storyline   c. An additional victim
  b. An additional killer   d. An additional survivor

180. In 2003, a comic titled what featured Lindsay Wallace as the main character?
  a. One Final Battle   c. One Last Chance
  b. One Good Scare   d. One Crazy Night

181. Michael Myers is one of several horror icons to be included in the 2009 version of the Universal Studios Hollywood's Halloween Horror Nights event as part of a maze titled what?
  a. Halloween: The Curse and Vengeance of Michael Myers
  b. Halloween: The Myth and Legend of Michael Myers
  c. Halloween: The Life and Crimes of Michael Myers
  d. Halloween: The Resurrection and Return of Michael Myers

182. Who wrote the novelization of the *Halloween 2 (1981)* film?
  a. Curtis Richards   c. Kelly O'Rourke
  b. Jack Martin   d. Nicholas Grabowsky

183. What was the name of the second *Halloween*-related book, yet unrelated to the film's timeline, that was released on December 1, 1997?
  a. The Old Myers House   c. The Old Myers Place
  b. The Old Myers Town   d. The Old Myers Sanitarium

184. Michael Myers makes an appearance as a playable character in which video game?
  a. Mortal Kombat   c. Street Fighter
  b. Dead by Daylight   d. Grand Theft Auto

185. Michael Myers can be downloaded as a playable character in which video game?
  a. WWE 2K17   c. Call of Duty: Ghosts
  b. Mortal Kombat   d. Call of Duty: Black Ops

186. Who voiced Michael Myers in the nineteenth episode of *Robot Chicken*?
  a. Joe Filippone
  b. John Rhys-Davies
  c. Seth Green
  d. Giancarlo Esposito

187. In a survey of the psychological appeal of movie monsters, it was published in the Journal of Media Psychology that Michael Myers was considered what?
  a. Embodiment of Horror
  b. Embodiment of Terror
  c. Embodiment of Pure Evil
  d. Embodiment of Pure Torture

188. What type of dog was Lester in *Halloween (1978)*?
  a. Pitbull
  b. Rottweiler
  c. German Shepherd
  d. Chocolate Lab

189. Which killer is Michael Myers associated with?
  a. Charles Manson
  b. Jack the Ripper
  c. OJ Simpson
  d. The Zodiac Killer

190. What garage did the truck driver work for that Michael killed in *Halloween (1978)*?
  a. Phillips Garage
  b. Pats Garage
  c. Phelps Garage
  d. Peters Garage

191. What medicine did Dr. Loomis tell Marion to give to Michael when they took him before the judge in *Halloween (1978)*?
  a. Thorazine
  b. Codeine
  c. Morphine
  d. Motrin

192. In *Halloween (1978)*, what two movies did Tommy and Lindsay watch over the night?
  a. The Thing and The Fog
  b. The Thing and Psycho
  c. The Thing and Alien
  d. The Thing and Forbidden Planet

193. In *Halloween 2 (1981)*, what movie were the Elrod's watching?
  a. Halloween
  b. Night of the Living Dead
  c. The Thing
  d. Friday the 13th

194. What was the novelty store that Dr. Loomis passed when in the Marshal's car in *Halloween 2 (1981)*?
  a. The Keepsake
  b. Jeepers Creepers
  c. Jonathan's Boutique
  d. Larry's Prank Store

195. When Nurse Karen Bailey wanted into the hospital, what movie was Mr. Garrett watching in *Halloween 2 (1981)*?
   a. Bram Stoker's Dracula
   b. Abbott and Costello Meet Frankenstein
   c. Dementia
   d. 20,000 Leagues Under the Sea

196. What year was Santa Mira founded as told in *Halloween 3: Season of the Witch*?
   a. 1885   c. 1888
   b. 1887   d. 1882

197. In *Halloween 3: Season of the Witch*, what type of community was Santa Mira?
   a. Irish Potato Patch
   b. Irish Amish Community
   c. Irish Farming Town
   d. Irish Ghetto

198. Who wrote the novelization of the *Halloween 4: The Return of Michael Myers* film?
   a. Jack Martin   c. Nicholas Grabowsky
   b. Curtis Richards   d. Kelly O'Rourke

199. How much did the *Halloween* franchise approximately make in the box office through international sales?
   a. $87,600,126   c. $73,343,992
   b. $91,228,341   d. $66,332,787

200. What was the name of the third *Halloween*-related book, yet unrelated to the film's timeline, that was released on February 1, 1998?
   a. The Funhouse   c. The Haunted House
   b. The Greenhouse   d. The Mad House

Part 11: Word Search

Find the words located in the word bank in the puzzle below.

```
R E B H A D D O N F I E L D P
D E H S G H C L I N I C N C S
K A A G S A M H A I N R F O A
H T N L B U T R U F D M J S N
C M M G T A Z B K U R P Y T I
R A B H E O B H X Q W E E U T
P C O P H R R Y O D N Y V M A
A F O U V A T F S S X C I E R
R J G M L T L A A I P G L S I
T I E P B H M L I I T I R O U
I Y Y K E O A W O N K T T T M
E C M I W R S F U W M F E A K
S L A N L N K P G Y E E N R L
V W N S A R S B O J M E N A Y
K I D J O Z N A S X L M N T A
```

Dangertainment	Babysitter	Haddonfield	Sanitarium
Halloween	Pumpkins	Costumes	Hospital
Samhain	Clinic	Realtor	Boogeyman
Parties	Masks	Thorn	Evil

Answer Key

Halloween (1978)

1. B	35. A	69. B
2. D	36. B	70. A
3. A	37. C	71. C
4. A	38. A	72. A
5. C	39. A	73. C
6. C	40. A	74. D
7. C	41. B	75. B
8. B	42. B	76. A
9. D	43. D	77. B
10. C	44. C	78. B
11. B	45. C	79. C
12. A	46. B	80. C
13. A	47. A	81. D
14. A	48. A	82. A
15. C	49. C	83. D
16. C	50. C	84. A
17. A	51. C	85. D
18. C	52. D	86. A
19. C	53. B	87. B
20. D	54. A	88. B
21. B	55. A	89. C
22. B	56. A	90. C
23. C	57. B	91. B
24. C	58. C	92. D
25. C	59. C	93. D
26. D	60. B	94. B
27. A	61. D	95. C
28. B	62. D	96. A
29. C	63. D	97. C
30. B	64. D	98. D
31. B	65. C	99. A
32. A	66. C	100. C
33. C	67. A	
34. A	68. C	

Halloween 2 (1981)

1. C	35. A	69. A
2. C	36. C	70. B
3. C	37. B	71. B
4. C	38. B	72. D
5. C	39. C	73. C
6. A	40. C	74. C
7. B	41. A	75. C
8. D	42. A	76. A
9. B	43. D	77. A
10. C	44. B	78. D
11. B	45. A	79. C
12. B	46. B	80. C
13. D	47. B	81. C
14. A	48. A	82. B
15. A	49. A	83. B
16. C	50. B	84. B
17. D	51. B	85. C
18. C	52. C	86. C
19. D	53. C	87. C
20. B	54. A	88. C
21. C	55. D	89. A
22. C	56. B	90. A
23. B	57. B	91. B
24. C	58. C	92. D
25. D	59. B	93. D
26. A	60. C	94. B
27. A	61. A	95. C
28. B	62. C	96. C
29. C	63. C	97. A
30. C	64. D	98. B
31. D	65. B	99. C
32. B	66. B	100. C
33. C	67. B	
34. A	68. C	

Halloween 3: Season of the Witch

1. D	35. B	69. B
2. A	36. A	70. B
3. B	37. D	71. A
4. C	38. C	72. A
5. C	39. B	73. B
6. C	40. B	74. D
7. A	41. C	75. C
8. A	42. C	76. D
9. D	43. D	77. C
10. C	44. D	78. B
11. B	45. C	79. A
12. D	46. A	80. A
13. A	47. B	81. A
14. B	48. C	82. A
15. A	49. A	83. A
16. C	50. C	84. C
17. C	51. C	85. D
18. D	52. A	86. D
19. B	53. A	87. A
20. B	54. C	88. B
21. C	55. D	89. C
22. C	56. D	90. C
23. D	57. A	91. B
24. B	58. C	92. D
25. A	59. A	93. C
26. D	60. C	94. B
27. B	61. A	95. A
28. C	62. C	96. A
29. C	63. A	97. C
30. A	64. A	98. C
31. A	65. B	99. C
32. D	66. C	100. C
33. D	67. A	
34. B	68. A	

Halloween 4: The Return of Michael Myers

1. A	35. B	69. B
2. A	36. C	70. C
3. C	37. C	71. C
4. C	38. B	72. A
5. D	39. B	73. D
6. D	40. C	74. A
7. B	41. A	75. B
8. B	42. C	76. C
9. C	43. A	77. B
10. C	44. D	78. D
11. A	45. C	79. A
12. A	46. C	80. B
13. D	47. A	81. B
14. C	48. C	82. A
15. C	49. B	83. B
16. A	50. B	84. C
17. D	51. A	85. B
18. B	52. C	86. B
19. B	53. B	87. B
20. B	54. C	88. C
21. A	55. B	89. B
22. A	56. D	90. C
23. A	57. C	91. C
24. C	58. A	92. D
25. C	59. C	93. C
26. B	60. C	94. C
27. D	61. C	95. A
28. A	62. C	96. B
29. D	63. B	97. A
30. B	64. B	98. D
31. D	65. D	99. D
32. C	66. A	100. C
33. D	67. B	
34. D	68. C	

Halloween 5: The Revenge of Michael Myers

1. D	35. A	69. C
2. D	36. B	70. C
3. B	37. C	71. D
4. B	38. B	72. A
5. D	39. A	73. D
6. C	40. B	74. D
7. A	41. D	75. D
8. C	42. D	76. B
9. C	43. B	77. C
10. A	44. C	78. C
11. D	45. C	79. C
12. D	46. A	80. C
13. B	47. A	81. D
14. B	48. C	82. A
15. B	49. C	83. B
16. B	50. C	84. A
17. A	51. C	85. B
18. C	52. B	86. C
19. C	53. B	87. B
20. A	54. C	88. B
21. C	55. D	89. B
22. A	56. B	90. D
23. C	57. C	91. A
24. C	58. C	92. A
25. C	59. A	93. A
26. D	60. A	94. D
27. C	61. C	95. C
28. B	62. C	96. A
29. D	63. B	97. A
30. A	64. D	98. A
31. B	65. D	99. D
32. C	66. C	100. C
33. C	67. B	
34. A	68. C	

Halloween: The Curse of Michael Myers

1. A	35. A	69. B
2. C	36. C	70. B
3. C	37. B	71. B
4. B	38. C	72. C
5. C	39. B	73. C
6. C	40. B	74. D
7. C	41. D	75. C
8. B	42. C	76. B
9. D	43. C	77. D
10. A	44. B	78. A
11. A	45. C	79. A
12. D	46. C	80. A
13. B	47. C	81. A
14. C	48. B	82. C
15. B	49. D	83. B
16. A	50. B	84. C
17. A	51. A	85. C
18. D	52. C	86. A
19. B	53. B	87. D
20. A	54. A	88. D
21. C	55. B	89. A
22. A	56. B	90. A
23. C	57. C	91. A
24. B	58. A	92. B
25. B	59. D	93. D
26. C	60. C	94. C
27. A	61. A	95. C
28. D	62. A	96. C
29. D	63. A	97. D
30. D	64. A	98. A
31. D	65. B	99. A
32. B	66. C	100. B
33. D	67. A	
34. A	68. B	

Halloween H20: 20 Years Later

1. C	35. C	69. A
2. C	36. C	70. B
3. C	37. B	71. B
4. C	38. C	72. C
5. C	39. C	73. D
6. A	40. C	74. A
7. B	41. C	75. A
8. D	42. C	76. A
9. C	43. B	77. B
10. C	44. D	78. D
11. D	45. D	79. D
12. B	46. C	80. D
13. A	47. A	81. D
14. B	48. C	82. A
15. B	49. A	83. C
16. C	50. C	84. D
17. C	51. B	85. C
18. C	52. B	86. A
19. C	53. B	87. C
20. B	54. C	88. A
21. B	55. D	89. A
22. A	56. B	90. A
23. A	57. A	91. B
24. A	58. A	92. C
25. D	59. B	93. D
26. A	60. D	94. A
27. B	61. A	95. B
28. C	62. B	96. A
29. D	63. B	97. D
30. A	64. C	98. A
31. B	65. D	99. A
32. A	66. C	100. A
33. B	67. B	
34. A	68. D	

Halloween: Resurrection

1. D	35. B	69. B
2. C	36. C	70. A
3. A	37. C	71. D
4. A	38. A	72. C
5. D	39. D	73. C
6. C	40. B	74. B
7. B	41. A	75. C
8. A	42. C	76. C
9. D	43. A	77. B
10. B	44. B	78. B
11. C	45. A	79. A
12. C	46. C	80. A
13. C	47. A	81. C
14. A	48. B	82. D
15. C	49. D	83. D
16. A	50. D	84. B
17. D	51. D	85. C
18. B	52. B	86. A
19. B	53. C	87. C
20. B	54. A	88. A
21. C	55. C	89. D
22. C	56. A	90. C
23. C	57. D	91. C
24. A	58. B	92. C
25. C	59. C	93. B
26. C	60. B	94. C
27. B	61. A	95. A
28. D	62. B	96. B
29. A	63. C	97. C
30. D	64. C	98. C
31. A	65. B	99. C
32. A	66. C	100. D
33. A	67. A	
34. C	68. C	

Halloween (2007)

1. C	35. A	69. A
2. A	36. A	70. A
3. C	37. B	71. B
4. C	38. C	72. C
5. C	39. D	73. A
6. B	40. D	74. C
7. D	41. B	75. B
8. A	42. A	76. B
9. B	43. C	77. C
10. A	44. C	78. A
11. C	45. A	79. A
12. C	46. B	80. C
13. B	47. B	81. D
14. C	48. C	82. D
15. C	49. A	83. C
16. D	50. C	84. C
17. D	51. C	85. B
18. D	52. B	86. A
19. C	53. D	87. A
20. C	54. C	88. A
21. C	55. C	89. B
22. C	56. A	90. D
23. A	57. C	91. D
24. D	58. A	92. B
25. A	59. B	93. C
26. B	60. D	94. C
27. C	61. B	95. B
28. A	62. B	96. C
29. A	63. C	97. C
30. C	64. A	98. D
31. A	65. D	99. D
32. D	66. C	100. C
33. B	67. C	
34. A	68. C	

Halloween 2 (2009)

1. D	35. C	69. D
2. D	36. A	70. C
3. D	37. C	71. A
4. D	38. B	72. C
5. D	39. C	73. D
6. A	40. A	74. B
7. A	41. C	75. D
8. B	42. C	76. A
9. B	43. B	77. C
10. A	44. C	78. A
11. C	45. C	79. B
12. C	46. C	80. A
13. D	47. C	81. B
14. A	48. B	82. A
15. B	49. D	83. D
16. A	50. A	84. A
17. C	51. A	85. A
18. C	52. A	86. B
19. C	53. D	87. D
20. A	54. A	88. A
21. B	55. C	89. C
22. A	56. B	90. C
23. A	57. B	91. C
24. D	58. A	92. A
25. B	59. C	93. C
26. C	60. C	94. B
27. A	61. C	95. D
28. D	62. C	96. A
29. A	63. B	97. A
30. D	64. A	98. A
31. C	65. A	99. C
32. C	66. B	100. C
33. B	67. C	
34. B	68. A	

Halloween (2018)

1. D	35. A	69. A
2. D	36. A	70. C
3. D	37. A	71. A
4. D	38. D	72. B
5. D	39. D	73. D
6. C	40. B	74. A
7. B	41. C	75. B
8. A	42. A	76. B
9. A	43. B	77. C
10. A	44. D	78. A
11. C	45. D	79. C
12. C	46. D	80. A
13. B	47. A	81. D
14. A	48. D	82. C
15. A	49. A	83. D
16. C	50. A	84. A
17. B	51. C	85. D
18. C	52. A	86. A
19. D	53. A	87. C
20. B	54. D	88. A
21. A	55. A	89. D
22. C	56. C	90. A
23. C	57. B	91. B
24. C	58. B	92. C
25. C	59. C	93. B
26. B	60. B	94. D
27. C	61. B	95. A
28. B	62. B	96. B
29. B	63. D	97. D
30. B	64. B	98. B
31. B	65. D	99. B
32. D	66. A	100. A
33. B	67. C	
34. D	68. D	

Halloween Mashup

Part 1: Word Scramble

1. Scream Queen
2. Haddonfield
3. Thorn
4. Halloween
5. Michael Myers
6. Evil
7. Silver Shamrock
8. Butcher Knife
9. Rabbit In Red
10. Dangertainment
11. October
12. Boogeyman
13. Babysitting
14. The Shape
15. The Clinic

Part 2: Who Am I?

16. Jamie Lloyd
17. Deborah Myers
18. John Strode
19. Mrs. Alves
20. Conal Cochran
21. The Kupfer Family
22. Tina Williams
23. Darlene Carruthers
24. Dr. Terrence Wynn
25. Brady
26. Michael Myers
27. Mrs. Blankenship
28. Lynda Van Der Klok
29. Dr. Hoffman
30. Buddy

Part 3: Fill in the Blank

31. Homecoming
32. Sundae
33. William Shatner
34. Lester
35. Max
36. Mayonnaise
37. Tree Branch
38. 1963
39. Illinois
40. Jamie Lloyd
41. Syringe
42. Piano
43. Pink
44. Devil
45. Deckard

Part 4: Hidden Character

46. Boogeyman
47. Evil
48. Crispy
49. Hell
50. Treat
51. House
52. Lessons
53. Home
54. Nearly
55. Jamie's
56. Sheriff
57. Scare

Hidden Character: Michael Myers

Part 5: True or False

58. B
59. B
60. B
61. A

62. A
63. A
64. B
65. A

Part 6: This or That

66. A
67. A
68. B
69. A
70. A
71. B
72. B
73. A

74. B
75. B
76. B
77. A
78. A
79. B
80. B

Part 7: Matching

81. B
82. H
83. F
84. I
85. A

86. J
87. D
88. G
89. E
90. C

Part 8: Who Said It?

91. Jamie Lloyd
92. Harry Grimbridge
93. Ronnie
94. Deborah Myers
95. Barry Simms

96. Mrs. Blankenship
97. Deputy Gary Hunt
98. Will Brennan
99. Marion Chambers
100. Kelly Meeker

Part 9: Who Played Who?

101. Ellie Cornell	118. Anne Bruner	135. George Sullivan
102. Tamara Glynn	119. Brent Le Page	136. John Zenda
103. Stacey Nelkin	120. Robert Curtis Brown	137. Joseph Gordon-Levitt
104. Josh Hartnett	121. Katee Sackhoff	138. Ana Alicia
105. Sasha Jenson	122. Janet Leigh	139. Haig Sutherland
106. Tawny Moyer	123. Danny Trejo	140. Kim Darby
107. Sean Whalen	124. Susan Swift	141. Marianne Hagan
108. Devin Gardener	125. Keith Bogart	142. Pamela Susan Shoop
109. Adam Arkin	126. Bradford English	143. Ryan Merriman
110. Kathleen Kinmont	127. Garn Stephens	144. Jonathan Terry
111. Sean Patrick Thomas	128. Matthew Walker	145. Wendy Wessberg
112. Gloria Gifford	129. Nancy Kyes	146. Maidie Norman
113. Jeffrey Landman	130. Leo Rossi	147. Howard Hesseman
114. Michael Pataki	131. Lucille Benson	148. Max Van Ville
115. Matt Bush	132. Carmen Filpi	149. Octavia Spencer
116. Tyra Banks	133. Ford Rainey	150. Karen Alston
117. Mitchell Ryan	134. Janice Knickrehm	

Part 10: Multiple Choice

151.	C	168.	C	185.	C
152.	C	169.	C	186.	C
153.	C	170.	B	187.	C
154.	D	171.	D	188.	C
155.	C	172.	A	189.	B
156.	B	173.	C	190.	C
157.	B	174.	D	191.	A
158.	D	175.	C	192.	D
159.	C	176.	B	193.	B
160.	A	177.	D	194.	A
161.	A	178.	A	195.	C
162.	D	179.	C	196.	B
163.	B	180.	B	197.	C
164.	B	181.	C	198.	C
165.	B	182.	B	199.	A
166.	C	183.	C	200.	D
167.	C	184.	B		

Part 11: Word Search

Dangertainment	Babysitter	Haddonfield	Sanitarium
Halloween	Pumpkins	Costumes	Hospital
Samhain	Clinic	Realtor	Boogeyman
Parties	Masks	Thorn	Evil